When I was five we lived in the house on the hill. I ... ... place: an old New E... ... house surrounded by a ... ... high grassy meadow ... ... the river and the town ... ... over side, the land tumbled away down a cliff—a craggy granite ledge which a former owner had equipped with a Victorian iron railing and a crudely cut path and steps. I would imagine I was one of the ladies with a parasol in my grandmother's photographs as I tripped along the path in delicately heeled high-button shoes, carrying the train of my traveling costume. It was our favorite way to reach the road below and provided wonderful sites for hide-and-seek! Deep in the wood was a mica mine, treasure in the heart of darkness! Standing behind the house, a row of tall pines, giant pines to a five-year-old! A broad swing with ropes reached up into the sky... the smell of pine needles and the sense of height, the soaring whoosh! of pine boughs, and the dizzy motion of ecstatic swinging all come back to me when I remember the house on the hill. We lived there only one year while the church found a parsonage on a more sedate and prestigious street. But for me, the house on the hill with its atmosphere of links to the past and to nature, its elevation above the town and in my mind above the river will always be the seat of childhood fantasy, filled with the sounds and color and scents of imagination, the

This book (and other Soleil Press publications about lifewriting, including books, manuals, workbooks, and binders for teachers and individuals who write personal and family histories) is available at volume discount for bulk purchase. For details, please contact Soleil Press at the address below.

PRINTED IN U.S.A.

THIRD EDITION

S O L E I L ✳ P R E S S

95 GOULD ROAD, #14 LISBON FALLS, MAINE 04252

207-353-5454

photoscribe@turningmemories.com

Visit our website: www.turningmemories. com

PUBLISHERS CATALOGUING IN PUBLICATION DATA
Ledoux, Denis
The Photo Scribe, A Writing Guide/How to Write the Stories
    Behind Your Photographs
1. Creative Writing.-2. Autobiography.-3. Crafts
I.Title
ISBN: 978-0-9742773-1-8
LC # 98-090625

BOOK DESIGN: Martha Blowen
INTERIOR PHOTOS: Thanks to Sally Lunt, Jill Grogg, Amy Grogg, Posey Lippincott, and Ledoux and Blowen families.
SPECIAL THANKS to Maxim Blowen-Ledoux

The Photo Scribe

A Writing Guide

How to Write the Stories Behind Your Photographs

by Denis Ledoux

Acknowledgements

Sally Lunt helped produce both the first and second editions of *The Photo Scribe* and this third one. We are grateful for her many talents, not the least of which are optimism and efficiency.

A number of Turning Memories Into Memoirs™ teachers and workshop leaders were kind enough to read and comment on advance copies of this manuscript when it was first published in 1998. Their insight and generosity are much appreciated. They are Rae Luckie, of Kiama, New South Wales; Dianne Aoki, of Honolulu, Hawaii; Carole Cole, of Bountiful, Utah; Margaret De Angelis, of Harrisburg, Pennsylvania; Jim O'Leary, of Albuquerque, New Mexico; and Audrienne Womack, of Washington, D.C.

Our special thanks will ever go to Ladora and Lucille, and to Maxim and Zoé, the generations who surround us with love and purpose and from whom we continue to learn every day.

—*D. L., M. B.*

Dedication

For the Creative Memories scrapbookers
I met in 1996 and 1997 in Minnesota
—their energy and enthusiasm for their work,
their willingness to freely share their spirit,
and their dedication to affirming and preserving
personal and family histories continues to inspire me.

And for
scrapbookers and families everywhere
who are preserving stories
in their lifestory photo albums.

—D.L.

Also by Denis Ledoux

Turning Memories Into Memoirs
A Handbook for Writing Lifestories

What Became of Them
and Other Stories from Franco-America

Mountain Dance and Other Stories

Lives In Translation: An Anthology of
Contemporary Franco-American Writings

Table of Contents

Preface

"My photos tell only a part of my family story. How can I include more of it in my albums?" scrapbook consultants asked when I presented writing workshops at two national Creative Memories™(CM) conventions. CM is an international company that promotes and teaches photo-safe*[1] scrapbooking awareness through classes and workshops.

My album looks great. Now I want it to tell the story I remember when I look at it.

Since 1988, I have helped thousands of people to write their personal and family lifestories* through my Turning Memories Into Memoirs™ workshops. Because of my experience, CM invited me to teach their consultants what scrapbookers call photojournaling. I taught them how to write interesting and effective narrative texts–cameo narratives*, I call them–to incorporate into the well-designed, photo-safe photograph albums they produce and advocate.

CM consultants were eager to add new skills to their album-making. They knew instinctively that learning to write more than a brief caption would satisfy their own needs to tell more complete stories and would enhance their work with customers who longed to create family-legacy albums.

Consultants wanted to tell a complete lifestory (personal

1. Words marked with an asterisk(*) are defined in the Glossary (p.117), as well as within the text.

or family story)–but they wanted to do so in their albums, not in book-length autobiographies* or biographies* peo-

An autobiography in my albums–I never thought of my photos that way before.

ple often produce in my Turning Memories™ workshops. They were not, and didn't want to be, writers first and album-makers second.

"My photo albums are where I want to record my lifestory," they said. "How can I integrate more text into them and still have the photos be central to the album?"

This book answers that question. In *The Photo Scribe,* you, too, will learn to tell your lifestory, or, if you choose, portions of it, using both photographs and short, well-written texts.

I call the family legacy album that results from combining photographs and text the "lifestory photo album*." And I call the process of creating it "photoscribing*."

Introduction

Photos are the driving force behind the story told in most albums–no photo, no story. It shouldn't be that way! In *The Photo Scribe,* you will learn to tell a lifestory using the events and relationships of your life, not the photos you happen to have on hand, as your primary organizing element. This principle, more than any other presented in *The Photo Scribe,* will help you make meaningful lifestory photo albums using photos, captions*, and cameo narratives.

I wish had a picture of that moment. I wish there were a way I could keep that memory alive.

Telling Your Lifestory

Photos depict an external version of our lives. They capture only material, visual things–leaving the viewer to guess about the deeper, sometimes hidden meaning.

The complexities of a given situation or experience may seem too difficult or embarrassing to put into words–so we leave them out and stick to names and dates. Or, we let those parts of the story show up in the storyline we tell a friend–perhaps in an off-hand manner–as we leaf through the pages of the album. This oral shar-ing fills the need we have to communicate the more complex story, but the spoken words exist only briefly. Once we have finished speaking, the story is again at risk of being forgotten.

"I'll note you in my book of memory."
—Shakespeare

Your Stories Are at Risk

Let's say you have begun to place your photos in albums and have given some thought to arranging them on a well-designed page. Let's say you have been careful to label each picture with an identifying caption such as: "Simpson's Beach, 2005."

Every time you look at that photo of your time at the beach, a flood of memories washes over you. You recall that it was that day, as you watched a couple playing with their toddler, that you decided you were ready to have a child and to quit your unsatisfying job. Your experience of making that life decision that day at the shore is still vivid to you as you look at the familiar image.

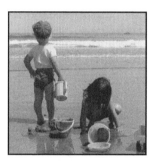

But the caption says only "Simpson's Beach, 2005." None of what was most significant about that time and place is recorded in your album. How can you, even if you want to, record a decision (or the feelings that went into it) in a photo? You can't! But, you *can* write a narrative* to put next to the photo.

On the beach, I watched a couple playing with their children. Their pleasure was so clear that I realized I wanted more than anything to be a parent, too. It was more important than the stressful career job at Nichols International I was trying to hold on to. Nothing but parenting seemed to matter after that beach day.

You'll notice that this cameo narrative is quite different from (and reveals a lot more than) the sort of comment line that reads:

Sun 'n' Sand. What a beach day!

Without a thoughtful narrative, the story of what was important at Simpson's Beach is a secret in the process of being lost-even though a well-preserved photograph presents the sun, the water, and the smile on your face. With the narrative, though, the vacation photo takes its place as a more complex record of a special time in your life and a turning point in your family's history.

I've changed so much! An old friend I met recently remembered me for things that aren't even a part of my life today!

What a meaningful story the photo and the narrative make to pass on to your children!

How The Photo Scribe Will Help

The Photo Scribe will help you to work as effectively with your story as you do with your photos-to crop story details, design a background of family facts and history, and add the "off-camera" elements to explain and enhance the storytelling in your album.

In photoscribing, you have two approaches for telling the complete stories of your photos:

1. You can tell the story that lies behind individual photos. In this book, you'll find techniques for uncovering and writing down the layers of details and background info the camera didn't capture. You can do this for single photographs without telling a longer story.

For example, you have a single photo that shows all your aunts and uncles on Gran's sofa, every face beaming a smile that says "family harmony." But this was the last holiday before the argument between them kept you from seeing your cousins for years. When you see that photo, you want to tell about that break and how it made you feel. Isn't that the story behind the photo you need to write, not just the happy story the picture tells?

Most pictures, as time goes by, turn their stories into secrets. We know from seeing odd artifacts at yard sales that one era's familiar objects are another's curiosities. With this in mind, it is important to choose even a few pictures to photoscribe so people may know and cherish your personal and family history in the future.

Sometimes I look at photos of my relatives as young people and wonder what the untold stories are behind them.

2. You can create a lifestory photo album. Captions and cameo narratives expand on individual photos, but they can do more. They can join with photos to create a story that is larger than the sum of the individual texts and photos. This greater story is told in the lifestory photo album. Striving to create such an album is a more ambitious undertaking than writing individual texts, but it's not beyond your abilities.

What You Won't Learn Here

It is not the aim of *The Photo Scribe* to help you to do any of the following. This book will not teach you:

■ **to create a photo-safe album.** There are many excellent sources for this. I urge you to always use photo-safe materials to protect your precious photos and artifacts from deterioration. What's the point otherwise?

■ **to design page layouts.** I urge you to make your albums as attractive as possible and to develop a style that pleases you and expresses your unique taste. I caution you, however, not to allow your creativity to overpower your main purpose–to tell your story as you preserve your photos. It's just as significant and creatively rewarding to preserve stories as it is to preserve the images. The design and content need to go hand in hand. *The Photo Scribe* is a scrapbooker's companion to the many layout and design books now on the market.

■ **to develop long written texts.** If writing appeals to you and you want to write extended family histories and personal memoirs*, check out *Turning Memories Into Memoirs, A Handbook for Writing Lifestories.* (See Soleil Press Directory, p.119.) It focuses on tips and effective exercises for writing memoirs. You don't need long texts, however, to create a lifestory photo album.

EXERCISE

Take a minute to think about the goals for your photo albums. Do you want to create

1. one or more albums in which individual cameo narratives add meaning and interest here and there (but not necessarily everywhere)?

2. lifestory albums that are a comprehensive history of your life or your family's? This goal lets you photoscribe an autobiography or biography of any length or depth.

Good Luck

The Turning Memories™ lifewriting method has led ordinary people to become successful lifewriters since 1988. *The Photo Scribe* adapts Turning Memories™ techniques to album-making so that you can uncover, develop, and express in your own words the stories behind your photos.

You *can* succeed at writing richly detailed and interesting stories to complement your photographs and make your albums more meaningful. The work you are undertaking to photoscribe your album is important for you and for your family.

I wish you all the success and satisfaction I know you will find in photoscribing!

Points to Remember

■ Your photos hold stories that are at risk of being forgotten and lost.

■ You can preserve your stories in written narratives as well as in photos in order to convey their complexity.

■ You can use photoscribing techniques to write cameo narratives for individual photos or you can weave text and photos into a unified whole to create a lifestory album–the choice is yours.

■ This is not a book about page layout or design.

■ Photoscribing is fun, fulfilling, and important!

Chapter One

Before You Begin

Many of us can speak easily and even fluently about our experiences, but when we are asked to write them down, we suddenly become wordless.

That may be one reason that photo albums are so popular. No need to struggle with writing–the pictures say it all. Or, do they?

Photos, however interesting or well-preserved, cannot convey the meaning of your story over time. Think of the photographs in antique shops. Each unknown face that looks out at you once had a whole story–yet who tells, or knows, it now? Sure, you can see it's a wedding portrait, but were the couple in love? Did they have children? Did they live into old age together or die young? The photo is a mute remnant of a story once fully known. Without words, the story has already been lost.

Every unidentified face is a story lost, a whole life lived–but now forgotten.

Don't worry about your stories getting lost. With the *The Photo Scribe*, you can learn to:

■ **write clear, meaningful, and interesting narratives** that will continue to tell your story for as long as there is someone to read it.

■ **deepen and expand the stories behind the photos in your albums** by adding background information and interpretation.

■ **preserve the stories you have no pictures for** though you realize these stories, too, are so necessary for understanding who you are, who your family is.

Writing down the story behind your photographs–your lifestory or your family's–shouldn't intimidate you. Photoscribing can be as creative and as fulfilling as designing layouts or taking pictures. If you can learn to do these, you can learn to photoscribe.

Narratives in Your Photo Album

Your photo albums already have a narrative or storyline. Narrative can be told by

■ the few or the many photos you've collected.

■ the words you write.

■ a combination of both.

Your albums, even without words, already communicate a story of your life and of your family and friends as they appear in the images and scenes of your photos. This image-based narrative, however, is minimal because photos can capture only a small part of any story.

When you know your story, you know who you are.

There are also many gaps and omissions in the stories your albums tell: the camera wasn't handy, the film was damaged, or you just forgot to take a picture. Photoscribing allows you to fill these gaps and to elaborate on the image-based narrative.

There are two narrative forms photo scribes use to create lifestory photo albums that tell the whole story. They are the photo caption* and the cameo narrative.

1. Photo captions are the information labels placed near photos as brief phrases or bulleted lists. Captions provide the basic names and dates and serve as clues to the narrative of your story. You probably find it easy enough to write this sort of caption in your albums:

> Mom and her date going to senior prom at Central High, 1964

"*Photographs afford us a glimpse back in history.*"
—*Martha Stewart*

When you annotate* basic info like this in an album, you assure that the basic **who, what, when,** and **where** of a photo are not lost. *The Photo Scribe* will show you how to do more: how to write an effective photo caption in your own words and how to avoid the *clichés** that seem jazzy now but convey little meaning over time. (See pp. 48-49, 85-86.)

2. Cameo narratives are short narratives (usually 50–150 words long) that are paired with photos or created to fill the story gap where there is no picture. A bare-bones caption adds a bit to the story your photo already tells–but not much. The larger story involves the **why** and **how,** as well as the **who, what, when,** and **where.** Was this a "big date" for Amy and Danny or just a pleasant social evening? Were there hopes and dreams being played out that

"*The story is about you.*"
—*Horace*

night? Without a word-based narrative, the viewer–and that could be you in a few years–has to supply her own guesses about "prom night." She has access to none of the multiple layers of meaning that made up the unique story of Amy and Danny that night in 1964.

When you write a narrative to go with the photo of Amy in her pale blue dress and Danny in that dapper suit, you create a fuller, deeper account of that evening, an account that tells much more of the story as it was lived by the unique individuals who mean so much to you.

Who Are These Stories for?

Expression implies an audience–someone whose response and approval, whose cheering and appreciation we seek because sharing our lives adds to the significance of our experience. It's a fundamental human impulse to tell our stories–to someone.

Are your albums a work of self-expression (even of art)? Of course, they are! Are you preparing a photo album so you can put it away and never view it again? Not likely. Your work cries out for its audience–someone to witness the experience and insights it preserves, to applaud or to weep or to chuckle over your photos and stories.

Your most important audience, of course, is always yourself. Make albums of your life that please you!

It's wise to consider who that audience will be before you photoscribe. Your audience will (and should) influence **what** you tell and **how** you tell your story. You will create a different lifestory photo album for your parents, for instance, than for business colleagues at your husband's promotion dinner. Being aware of who will (or may) see which album as you sort your photos and plan your project will help you make the best choices.

Just because you write the story down doesn't mean it has to become public property.

EXERCISE

Different albums may have different audiences. For instance, a *heritage album* may be intended for your children when they become adults who will be more interested in family history than they are today at age 4 and 6. A *vacation album* may have two audiences: your family this winter reliving the warmth of the holiday and your children in the future wanting to understand their childhoods. A *theme album* may have non-family members as an audience—for instance, *a career album* you may display in your office.

1. Make a list of your intended audience(s). (Jen and Jason, future grandchildren, Dave's parents, etc.)

2. Make a list of the albums you want to work on. (Diane's Friends, Florida '07, Troop #116, etc.)

3. Match the lists as appropriate. What particular needs and interests will each audience have? What will your needs be?

Lifestory Albums Are Not Journals

When you photoscribe a lifestory photo album, you will always have to chose what to include and what to leave out as you record a much more detailed and complete account of your personal and family stories.

Unless you are a public figure, there is no public right to know anything about your life, present or past.

So how do you determine how deep you really want to go if your goal is to have your lifestory album(s) do more than reflect just the glossy surface of your story and yet retain privacy and dignity for yourself and for your family? Dealing with difficult stories will, after all, be very healing for you. (See Appendix B, p. 107, "Unsettling Memories.")

Knowing from the start that there are several alternatives to telling everything to anyone and everyone may help you

I advocate neither sharing everything with everyone nor turning every photo album into a lifestory album.

to feel more comfortable about writing down your stories. Here are suggestions on how to tell a fuller (if not always bare-your-soul complete) story to a chosen audience while maintaining privacy:

1. Create a second, slightly different album to be kept private when your material is too personal. Create a more traditional album with brief, informative captions for display. Make a duplicate lifestory album with more personal cameo narratives for you (and perhaps your family).

2. Store cameo narratives you want to keep private in a separate companion binder or envelope. Label it:

For Family Only: Additional narratives for lifestory photo albums. Whether your public scrapbook has references within its pages to this private binder or envelope is up to you. (For example, next to a photo, you can write, *See pp. 36-37 in For Family Only.* Of course, you can choose to make no reference at all.) When you opt for a separate binder for your more personal stories, there's no need to duplicate photos. The binder can be for stories only.

3. Take your too-personal lifestory albums out of public view. Keep them as you would your journals–in a private place. In that way, you can be certain that they will be out of bounds to anyone with whom you haven't chosen to share them.

"Memories are all we really own."
—*Elias Lieberman*

EXERCISE

Audience: Comfort vs. Communication

1. Answer these questions for each era, theme or person featured in your albums. Take your time and be specific.

▓ Is there anything you don't want to share about these eras, themes, persons? Why is sharing uncomfortable to you?

▓ What info (facts and feelings/understandings) might you have a responsibility to communicate to people of the future?

2. Fill in the blanks below. Other "what if's" may occur to you as you write. Answer these, too.

▓ If I told _____ about my family and

their _____ , s/he or they would

_____ .

▓ If _____ knew about the time that I

_____ , it would change the way

_____ .

▓ If the world knew that I _____ ,

I would feel like I ought to_____ .

3. If you keep a journal, write on the topic of your personal privacy threshold. Write for at least ten minutes.

Schedule for Success: Plan Ahead

Studies have shown that people who set specific goals–*and write them down*–accomplish more than people who don't. So I urge you to make and write down a schedule using the following options.

1. Create a schedule based on hours per week. How much time do you want to devote (or can you realistically spare) for photoscribing? Be specific: "two hours on Tuesdays and Thursdays from 9 to 11 A.M. while Emma's in pre-school" or "every weekday evening that I'm not out from 7 to 8 P.M."

2. Set a schedule based on a number of pages. Decide how many pages you want to complete in a week. Estimate how long it will take, then schedule that number of hours. You'll have to work beyond your scheduled hours if you haven't met your page quota! Or, you could quit once you produce your pages. (But, why not "bank" additional pages for a busy week coming up?)

The photoscribing work you are doing is important to you and your family. Plan for it as you would for any important project.

3. Set a deadline for finishing the task. For example, choose an upcoming holiday, a family reunion, a wedding. Tell people to expect your album on that date; their anticipation will keep you on task.

4. Make it a rule to "pay back" time you "borrow" before you "borrow" from your schedule again. Like financial debts, project debts can really add up!

Set Goals That Work for You

Photoscribing your albums may take a while! In order to accomplish your overall goal ("to photoscribe all my albums"), break that big goal down into intermediate ones ("to photoscribe my high school album by the reunion in June" and even "to write ten cameo narratives by next Friday"). Successfully meeting these smaller goals will encourage you to continue as you savor your success at regular intervals.

Keep these guidelines in mind.

1. Be realistic. Transforming your albums is a big job. You have many photos to collect, organize, and write about. Don't set self-defeating, unrealistic goals ("photoscribe all my albums in three months").

2. Settle on a pace you can maintain. It's an important project worth doing–and so are many others! Don't preserve your past at the expense of healthfully living your present!

3. Build breaks into your work. Allow yourself to let it go for a while and then return to the task.

4. Reward yourself for accomplishing intermediate goals. Share your work with friends and family who will be appreciative. Indulge in healthy "treats."

5. Don't force yourself to write about difficult times. Eras, people, or events you don't want to deal with don't have to be your first subjects. There may be some years you really don't want to docu- ment–at least not yet. Focus first on subjects that will bring the most satisfac- tion. You'll find difficult or sad times easier to write about if you learn the skills and experience the satisfaction by photoscribing happy times first! (See Appendix B, p. 107, for more informa- tion on dealing with unsettling memo- ries.)

"Mom was amazed. When I told her I was 'photoscribing,' she hadn't understood, but when she saw the album I made of Grandma and Gramps, she choked right up. She was so pleased that I cared so much!"

6. Be selective. You don't have to write a narrative for every photo in an album.

7. Share your work-in-progress. Show it to friends and family. Let their enthusiasm inspire you. But don't depend on others–praise yourself for work you have accomplished.

8. Establish the habit of organizing your photos as they come in. Label new photos right away to avoid turn- ing today's photos into tomorrow's mystery pictures. Keep a notebook for details and impressions.

9. Use a binder to organize your photoscribing pro- ject-in-process. Keep rough drafts, exercises, lists, and notes in a three-ring binder with dividers for each category. (*The Photo Scribe's Memory Binder* is designed just for this. See Soleil Press Directory, p. 119.)

Photo Safe Is Photo Smart

If you're going to preserve your photographs, invest in photo-safe materials that will last. Do it once, do it for good! Why create an album whose pages will destroy your photos–and your creative work–within a generation?

Can you afford *not* to record your personal and family history? It is one of your most valuable assets and an invaluable gift to the future.

Points to Remember

- Photoscribe your stories.
- Captions and cameo narratives expand on your photos and bridge the gaps between them.
- Audience influences your choice of what to write.
- Photoscribing doesn't mean making your private life public. How much you share is your choice.
- Make yourself a schedule. Plan it, share it with others, and then stick to it!
- Set realistic goals.
- Photo safe is always photo smart. It's worth the effort and expense to use materials that will last.

Chapter Two

The Lifelist

The life you (or your family or subject) have lived, not the photos you have available, is the organizing principle behind creating a meaningful lifestory photo album.

Writing cameo narratives that tell the story behind the photos of a lifetime, and that fill in the gaps in your photo collection, can be daunting–even when you're still relatively young and can devote many hours to the task. What you need is a guide that will make the task "do-able." The Lifelist* is such a guide. It will take you through the process of photoscribing your lifestory albums.

A Lifelist is a list of everything and anything you've ever done, said, thought, or felt, and of everyone and everything you've ever known in your life.

"Oh, my goodness," I can hear you saying. "You've got to be kidding–*everything?!!*"

Now don't panic and don't dismiss the idea before reading on. The Lifelist is a tool that will actually simplify your photoscribing process while it deepens the level of meaning in your albums.

Your Lifelist, whatever its type, must contain many detailed memories, of small as well as significant events and relationships.

Creating and working from a Lifelist will help you to:

■ **remember and record your life in more detail,**

■ **identify and prioritize events and interactions of your life** in order to record or feature them in your lifestory photo album,

■ **fill in the gaps between photos** with interesting and well-written cameo narratives,

Photoscribing without a Lifelist is like setting out on a trip without directions or a map.

■ **determine what story you tell** rather than let the story be dictated by the photos you happen to have. Your story should be enhanced, rather than limited, by your photos.

How to Compile Your Lifelist

The secret to success in compiling a Lifelist is to write down every memory that goes through your head. No kidding! Don't judge. Don't evaluate. Just keep writing down everything that pops into your head.

A Lifelist starts with slowing down your thoughts and allowing yourself to remember. Let your mind wander. Jot down whatever memories come up.

Making a lifestory album is a journey inward to your self and then outward to your family.

Write without reservation and just long enough to recall the memory clearly–as few as three to five words may be enough. Remembering or writing a lifelist chronologically is not necessary. Here are topics that appear on Lifelists:

■ early childhood memories,

■ first schooling,

■ the arrival of a sibling,

■ the community (town, street), the ethnic or religious group you grew up in,

■ fires, floods, tornadoes, accidents, or mishaps,

■ family illnesses, deaths,

■ important or influential relationships with relatives, an elder, or a peer,

■ failures or successes at high school, scholarships, a decision to go or not to go to the university, a conflict with a teacher, having to leave school for work,

■ boyfriends or girlfriends, deciding to marry or not,

■ career, training, work life, achievements,

■ friendships, colleagues,

■ home life, house life, family life, your children.

EXAMPLES
from my own lifelist circa 1963

■ annual ice festival
■ very serious about studying
■ using the language lab
■ binding books in the library
■ silence in the study halls
■ mail call at 10:40 A.M.
■ walking outside after classes
■ honor roll: 80 or better
■ ships docking downtown
■ learning Spanish
■ early winter darkness
■ emphasis on team sports
■ lights from the mill

Your list will eventually grow long and more detailed. It will even contain specific memories of a particular day or experience as well as more general memories of things you did and experienced many times. As part of "summers at the lake," you might write something like: *sitting on the green chair next to Mother; mollasses cookies; picking apples at Grandma's.*

People sometimes wonder if a certain memory is important enough to be included on a Lifelist. Don't worry if a certain memory is important or not. If you remember it, it's definitely important enough to go on your Lifelist. All your memories are important; all of them can be used in some way to inform (or give background to) successful and interesting narratives that you will tell in photo and text.

As you compile your Lifelist, memories will be jumbled—old ones next to new, important ones next to trivial. That's ok for now. Sorting is a separate, later task.

EXERCISE

1. Write down at least twenty memories (forty would be better, and eighty preferable) on your Lifelist. Use just three to five words for each. Write and remember uncritically. Chronology is not important at this stage.

2. Place this list in your Photo Scribe Memory Binder.

Lifelists—Long and Short

When you record memories of an entire lifetime on your Lifelist, you are producing an Extended Lifelist.* My

A Lifelist gets you to your destination: no missed turns or hours spent going down the wrong road!

example (p.29) is an excerpt from my Extended Lifelist. Eventually, yours will have several hundred or even as many as five hundred or more items. It's not unusual for people who are reviewing their entire lives to devote time over two or three weeks to this one task alone.

When doing a particular album, it's not necessary to compile an Extended Lifelist. A short list is needed. It's called the Limited Lifelist*.

The more memories, the more choice you have when you use your own unique Lifelist as a map to photoscribe your albums.

Do you want to work on an album of just one period (Zach's infancy), event (Mira's wedding), or theme (Bob's volunteer work) of your life or of the life of another person? When you create a Lifelist for one album, or even for several pages, you are generating a Limited Lifelist.

You may also want to elaborate parts of an Extended Lifelist into smaller, more detailed memories. When you focus on a smaller category of time, place, subject, or event, you are also creating a Limited Lifelist.

Let's look at the last topic on the Lifelist ("your children") on page 29. Here's how you might elaborate to focus on the birth of your second child in a Limited Lifelist:

E X A M P L E S

Jake's driver's license

- driver's ed in October
- Jake as our chauffeur
- winter driving hazards
- night driving practice
- parallel parking
- turning 16 in May
- insurance!
- THE DAY
- car-sharing!

■ recalled conversations with older child about the baby brother/sister to come,

■ preparing for the baby (be specific: clothes, crib, the first-born's bedtime routine),

■ classes, pre-natal care and care-givers, baby shower, friends and relatives,

■ the birth day itself, special details, the story,

■ reactions and adaptations from older child.

Now you have a map of this topic. Use it as a guide to tell the story in photos and narratives. Notice that you have not yet worked with photos. Remember: it is important to work with your memories *before* you work with your photos. Memory–your memory–is Step One in creating a complete lifestory photo album. Referring to your photos is Step Two.

EXERCISE

1. Choose one item from the Extended Lifelist you have begun.

2. Make a Limited Lifelist: write down on a separate piece of paper as many as ten specific component memories that you associate with that one general memory.

For instance, if you wrote *high school graduation,* now write: *Aunt Lil came for Baccalaureate, Mom had the flu that week, Nancy came from D.C., Posey's party, Wilma's chocolate cake, daisy chain, my gown was too short, Uncle Leo's call, gifts from Marianne.*

Keep at it!

Once you start actively recalling memories for a Lifelist, you will find that they surface at all sorts of moments: while you wait for a traffic light to turn, while you gaze out the window as you do the dishes, while you chat at a friend's house about your week.

Not all the memories on your Lifelist need to go in your lifestory album. Some will always be private.

Memories surface from the unconscious. When you forget something, it's because your unconscious has swallowed it up. The unconscious yields a memory only reluctantly–and snatches it back as quickly as possible. That's why we recall and quickly forget. Beat the unconscious: carry a small spiral notebook around in your pocket or purse to jot down memories as they come back to you. That way you won't forget–your memory will be in writing.

To create a lifestory album, you must first know your story and all its details.

After a while your Extended or even your Limited Lifelist may seem long. Don't quit! In fact, it's probably not long enough yet! Continue to add to it in the days and months ahead as more memories occur to you. Placed in your *Photo Scribe Memory Binder* with your narratives, your list helps organize your lifestory album. (See Soleil Press Directory, p. 119.)

EXERCISE

1. Review your Extended Lifelist.

2. On separate pieces of paper, make a Limited Lifelist for each of the topics that interests you. As you come across memories that belong to another topic, put them on that topic's page.

3. Work with these lists to make them useful. Add, delete, combine, or expand until you are satisfied. Some photoscribes focus on one topic at a time; others enjoy multi-tasking this Lifelist process. Either way, the Lifelist you create will assure that you maintain the storyline you want to preserve.

Memory Is Often Faulty

You may feel that you already know your story–after all, you are the one who has lived your life! The fact is most of us don't accurately remember stories–not even the ones we are so sure we do. What we "know" is a version that has evolved over the years through remembering and retelling. There is a lot to be said for the theory that we remember the memory and not the event!

Those old enough to have lived through the assassination of John Kennedy often say that "you can never forget where you were when you heard the news." Since then, unfortunately, there have been other similarly memorable events whose impact is so strong that individuals recall the experience even though they may have been far away from "ground zero."

"Memory is a very frail thing. The written word stands forever."
—M. Gandhi

One fall, on the anniversary of Kennedy's death, I told my children about my experience of hearing that startling news. Later, in the process of writing about memory, I went back to my journal of that time.

Neither the "when" nor the "where" I recalled when telling my story were correct according to the journal entry I wrote at the time! It's a study in itself to ponder how we recreate ourselves and our self-images by subtly, unconsciouly, altering our memories over time.

Don't assume your memory is reliable. Always cross-check your Lifelist facts with other people or with written resources (journals, old letters, newspaper clippings).

EXERCISE

If you are a journal keeper, you can easily confirm the faulty memory phenomenon:

1. **Recall an incident that occurred at least ten years ago.**

2. **Write down the details as you remember them.**

3. **Cross check your memories by going back to the journal where you recorded the incident; compare what you wrote then with what you've written now.**

I am confident that you will find some, perhaps even many, discrepancies in the two versions.

If you are not a journal keeper:

1. **Follow steps 1 and 2 above.**

2. **Then cross check your memories by**

   ■ **rereading old letters, newspaper clippings, diplomas, or other artifacts you may have.**

   ■ **asking others who were there what details they remember.**

3. **Now compare what you learned from your research with what you first wrote.** Does new or different information suggest that you should revise your list or account?

Points to Remember

- Compile your Lifelist uncritically. It is your basic tool for remembering and organizing a lifestory album.
- Work with your memories first and your photographs second.
- Lifelists can be Extended or Limited.
- Memory isn't always as accurate as we make it out to be.
- Verify names, dates, and details with a variety of sources.

Note to workshop leaders and teachers: The worksheet, Writing Great Memory Lists, *provides an extensive step–by–step exercise for developing a Lifelist. It greatly facilitates the task of teaching this aspect of photo-scribing. Please refer to the Soleil Press Directory for info (p. 119).*

Chapter Three

Working With Photographs

Your next step in making a lifestory photo album is to work with your photos. In this chapter, you will:

■ **get to know your photos.** Doing so will make it easier to write the stories behind them,

■ **expand your Lifelist.** It's time to let your pictures stimulate your memory so that you keep adding to your Lifelist,

■ **determine where the gaps are in your photograph collection.** You will fill these with additional photos or with cameo narratives.

Starting Points

Although you can start a lifestory photo album from anywhere on your Lifelist or in your photo collection, good choices for a beginner include:

■ **the last six months.** Events and details are fresh in your mind so documenting and cross-checking them will be easy. With details under control, you can practice the skills of creating a lifestory album.

Your memories and your thoughts about specific photos and your Lifelist are the tools you will use to craft both photo captions and cameo narratives.

■ **a distinct era** for which you have few photos. The photo selection process is minimal, and it is more evident and pressing to fill out the story line with words instead of photos.

■ **a period that has little emotional impact for you.** You may be afraid of the feelings associated with some photos. By working first with neutral images and unchallenging memories, you can learn the skills you need without confronting difficult content.

■ **a year for which you already have written material.** The process is more accessible when you use existing journal entries, letters, or vignettes* and stories that you have on hand.

■ **a special event** such as a wedding, graduation, or retirement. These can present a clearly defined focus.

Grouping Your Photos

Your photos are an important source of memories. They will help you fill out your Lifelist.

Group your photos in some way that makes sense to you. There are many ways you can do this, such as by:

■ **occasion** (Thanksgiving 2006),
■ **subject** (Scout Troop 101, '03-'04),
■ **time period** (Jake's baby photos),
■ **character** (Nana McGowan).

Sometimes as you group your photos, memories will surface that haven't before. Jot down these new memories on your Lifelist. (Remember not to censor any thoughts or feelings.)

"I was amazed at how many details and little moments from my past came back to me when I spent more time with my photographs!"

Dwell with the events and eras of your "go-together" photos. Simply linger with the photos. Look at them intently; stay with each photo or with groups of them.

Additional memories and feelings may arise. Record these on your Lifelist.

Go through your Lifelist and note which memories do not appear in any photographs. Writing these as cameo narrative topics will deepen and complement your pictures.

*It's frustrating to complete your album and **then** discover photos that could have deepened and, in some cases, altered a story in the album.*

Ask family and friends for copies of photos you don't have but wish you did. Record in your Lifelist any memories that arise.

EXERCISE

1. Surround yourself with photos of a period from which you want to recall more—or more detailed—memories. In your home, office, or wherever you spend large amounts of time, set them where you can see them daily—in a line on a table in your living room, tucked into a picture frame in the kitchen, resting on a lamp on your bureau.

2. As you look at these photos, you will find yourself remembering vividly what you see in the photo: "Oh, yes, my grandfather had that habit of always…" or "my mother wore that green winter coat forever."

These are "old" memories. By recalling them, however, you set the stage for remembering other details: how your father would say, "Nancy, go out and get a new coat," and how she would reply, "It's good enough to go another year." Suddenly, you have to admit how it wasn't just over the coat that your parents would quibble like this. As you allow this photo to evoke these familiar voices, you leave the "old" memories and find yourself in "new" ones. When you linger with your photos, you enter their world and remember things suggested by, but not specifically in, the photos you hold in your hand.

3. Add these memories to your Lifelist and place in your Photo Scibe Memory Binder.

Speaking Personally

Working with photos, I've often come across over-looked or lost elements. In one taken on the steps of my

grandparents' house, for instance, my mother squints into the bright sun. One day, I suddenly saw my grandmother's figure emerge from the background*. What had been a shadow was really a smiling grandmother! I've come to treasure that surprise behind the posed foreground*. "Oops," she seems to say, with a happy expression, "I didn't mean to step into the picture!" Because I lingered with this image (and no one had cropped the photo), I found her there. Doing so has allowed me to enjoy many memories.

By lingering with two other pictures, I caught a mistake in dates. In both, a child–clearly that cutie is me–is wearing a snowsuit. The second face is a bit indistinct. I wonder innocently why I don't look more like myself. Then I ask, why am I an infant in a photo taken in front of the Webster Street house? We moved there when I was three!

Then it clicks! I was certain–but wrong–because I ignored the evidence in the photo. That's my sister in the suit I'd outgrown. She was the baby when we lived in that house. How could I have missed it?

EXERCISE

Looking With New Eyes

1. Choose a number of photos (five at least) of one period or with one theme. Scrutinize them for answers to the following questions. Jot down the answers for future use.

■ What do the backgrounds in the photos tell us about the people in the photos?

■ What are their income levels? their tastes? their educations? their religious practices?

■ What do the things you see in the photograph tell you about daily life? Be sure to take into account such features as dress, shoes, eyeglasses, pets, yards, cars, neighborhoods, toys.

■ Are there members of the family or other people missing from the photos who, you think, should be there? Why are they not there?

■ By the way people are standing together or apart, turned toward or away from each other, can you "see" something significant about their relationships?

2. Be a detective: look at each photo and ask any and every question. What happened before and after the photo was taken? Why did these people come together for this occasion?

3. Search for hidden elements you had not noticed before even in recent photographs. Also ask yourself what the photos would tell you about yourself or your family if you were a stranger looking at them.

4. Note your feelings that emerge from viewing these photos. How do they inform you about yourself or the people shown?

5. Repeat this exercise and use your "new eyes" to find the hidden elements in every photo you include in your lifestory photo album. Scrutinize these photos for answers to the above questions. Have a pad of paper handy to jot down your answers for future reference.

Points to Remember

- Choose an era or an event that makes a workable starting point.
- Group your photos to stimulate your memory. Dwell with your groups of photos for a while–then add your thoughts, feelings, and memories to your Lifelist.
- Don't rush! Allow yourself the time to linger with the process.

Chapter Four

Writing Great Captions

Now that you've generated (at least part of) your Lifelist and have grouped your photos, it's time to start writing the text for your lifestory album(s).

A photo scribe's two basic writing tools are the caption and the cameo narrative. While longer autobiographical essays can be effective in albums or as separate books (and I encourage you to write full memoirs if this interests you), this book doesn't address that process. (See *Turning Memories Into Memoirs*, Soleil Press Directory, p.119.) Longer writing is not necessary for a lifestory album.

Just a Few Words

Captions are identifications or brief tags that you write to accompany your photos. They are essential to your albums because they establish:

■ **a cast of characters***: mother, grandfather, your children as babies, friends. (Identifications are important as appearances change over time.)

■ **an action** (plot*): scenes at a wedding or graduation. (In some photos, the bride or the graduate aren't there; years later, when you look at these smiling, well-dressed people, what makes the occasion clear? Why did the people gather?)

■ **a setting***: this city, not that one; this year, not that year; this event, not that one; this cultural background, not that one. (Again, will such distinctions be identifiable years from now?)

You don't need to write: "This photo is about. . ." Just jump in with the details.

Remember that captions, while they furnish character, action, and setting, also provide much more information:

■ **Who is in the photo?** Include the full names and the relationships of characters to each other and to you: *Aunt Mary (Donaldson), my mother's sister.*

■ **What is portrayed in the photo?** Include both action and setting of the occasion and any background description: *wedding reception for Stephanie Donaldson Martin (Mary's daughter).*

Here you can also include extra information: *Aunt Mary made Steph's wedding gown.*

■ **Where (in what setting) does the action occur?**

Include names of buildings, streets, cities, states: *at the Knights of Columbus Hall, Broad Avenue, Grand Rapids, Michigan.*

■ **When does the event occur?** This is setting and it refers to the time. Include year, date and day as appropriate: *Saturday, June 23, 1973.*

■ **What else was going on** (action) in the family or the individual's life: *Aunt Mary was recovering from the heart attack she'd had in April.*

Finished captions do not separate the basic elements as I do above to illustrate this point. Because I wanted to make clear the distinctions of who, what, where, and when,

I wrote separate sentences for each. For an album, I would write these into one caption:

> Aunt Mary (O'Connell Donaldson), my mother's sister, at her daughter Stephanie's (Donaldson Martin) wedding reception, Knights of Columbus Hall, Grand Rapids, Saturday, June 23, 1973. Although she was recovering from a heart attack in April, she made Steph's wedding gown, including the embroidery on the bodice.

The information in this "Aunt Mary caption" is important and should be included on an album page, but the details needn't be featured with every photo or even with every cluster of photos of that event. You don't need to repeatedly identify Aunt Mary on subsequent pages (but you should label the back of each and every picture with a photo-safe pencil in case it is ever separated from the album).

If a number of years have passed since someone last appeared in your album, it's best to identify them. Your kids, not as familiar with Aunt Mary as you are, may not recognize her at a different time of her life.

EXERCISE

1. Select a page of your album or a few photos.

2. Write captions that provide the who, what, where, and when that pertain to each photo.

3. As you do so, write specific, proper words: "Aunt Mary" not "an aunt"; "the Knights of Columbus Hall, Grand Rapids, MI" not "a rented hall." For another photo, you might write:

"Popham Beach" not "at the shore;" or

"3rd grade at Marion T. Morse School" not "early school years."

As they go through your albums, your family and friends should be able to trace your life from person to person, from place to place, from time to time. Be clear and specific with your information in order to preserve the whole story.

Tips for Writing Captions

In an album, the basic who, what, where, and when captions are essential for identifying people, places, and things. Captions, even short ones, can also provide opportunities to:

■ **write from the heart.** Write the words that say what you feel! Let yourself be poetic and romantic. Let your imagination soar!

I remember spending hours just looking at you when you were a new baby. It felt like we were still one, and my whole life was brand new just like you.

■ **write with candor.** Just say it. Let yourself write what you want to write. Express all your love and admiration, your hopes and understandings, your thoughts and your experience.

People always stopped to talk with him when we went into town–he was so well-liked! He was so different at home where he spent hours in his study, silent and alone.

■ **write with details.** Use your senses. Describe a sight, a taste, a sound, a smell, the feel of something in the photo in specific details.

The rain scattered the glowing red and yellow leaves across the slippery black road. As we walked, we could smell frost-bitten, rotting leaves and the wet pavement smell of autumn.

■ **write simply.** Don't go looking for big words. The vocabulary you have right now is just fine. There's no need to try to be fancy or deep. Sometimes the surface is all right because it's surface you need to tell.

We left at 10 P.M., and by 7:30 the next morning, we were at Linda's eating breakfast at her kitchen table overlooking the lake.

■ **write your impressions.** Photo captions are your chance to express your take on life itself and on your life and your family's in particular.

> Those were our happiest years. It seemed like we were all working on the same thing for the same purpose. I'd go back to those days anytime!

"My task...is, by the power of the written word, to make you hear, to make you feel—it is, before all, to make you see. That, and no more—and it is everything."
—Joseph Conrad

E X E R C I S E

1. Review albums you have previously created and evaluate at least 10 captions.

2. Rewrite them, if necessary, asking yourself if you have written:

from the heart, with candor, with details, with simplicity, with your impressions.

Problem Captions

While captions present you with many opportunities to make an effective album, they can also drag your albums down if you're not aware of potential problems. These can include:

1. meaningless prose that fills space without much thought. You might be tempted to write for photos of an ocean vacation, *The ocean was so beautiful!*

While you might say, "But, that's how I feel. The ocean *was* beautiful!" there is much more feeling and experience to explore and share. For instance, how does the ocean make you feel: rested or restless, centered or isolated, connected to the universe or uneasy? What affects you: sound, light, color, the movement of the waves, the open space?

Avoid meaningless writing by taking the time to linger with your photos. Re-enter the time when the pictures were

taken, and recall the feelings and features of your life at that time.

In writing a caption for that ocean photo, ask yourself, "What did this vacation mean to me?" or "How was I specifically affected by being in that place at that time?" As a result of these and similar questions, you might write one of the two captions that follow in your album:

Jan and I were finally able to drop our roles as business partners and be a couple again in those two weeks on Monhegan.

Water is my element—once again I found that being at the ocean restored me in a way that mountains and forests never do.

2. borrowed phrases. These predictable, uninformative, and generally uninteresting tags are *A mocking voice is an* also called *cliché*. For instance, for a *album convention from* photo of you working in the garden why *the past that doesn't serve* write a flippant caption like:
the photo scribe well.
> ■ *A girl's work is never done!*
■ *Where's the sun block?!*
■ *I love to get my hands dirty.*
■ *Oh, my nails!*

Think of yourself 10 years from now looking at the photo of you working in the garden. (Even more, imagine your grown children in 20 years!) What will flippant captions say about who you were and what you were doing? What can cute captions contribute to the making of a lifestory photo album? Not much!

Every caption you write in your albums can be interesting, meaningful, and satisfying to read–and reread, as you return to them again and again. All it takes is attention to detail and a commitment to the future (qualities you already have or you wouldn't be reading this book!).

Now think of your garden photo annotated with something like this:

Clichés will never tell you or your children's children the meaningful story behind the photograph.

> The previous year, I began composting all our kitchen and yard waste and the garden absolutely bloomed! It was my best garden to date.

or

> I enjoyed gardening that summer and I was good at it (note the five different types of lettuce lower right)!

3. repeated information already in the photo. For a picture of your kids in a treehouse, why write, *The kids at the treehouse.* Instead, use the opportunity to say something, in your own words, about these wondrously unique kids of yours that is not already obvious from the picture.

> As usual, Ryan had big plans and Kayla kept calling out cautions. Ryan liked working alone but Kayla wanted Dad to help.

> Kayla and Ryan usually have very different play styles but they sure worked well together on this project! And they played in the treehouse all summer.

Imagine your grandchildren, years from now, reading, *the kids at the treehouse,* or one of the longer captions above. Which will be more satisfying to them?

When what is going on in the photo is not entirely obvious, then stating it clearly in the caption is in order. Fabric spread out on a table doesn't say what is being cut out or why. *Making shower curtains for the new bathroom* then becomes an important piece of information.

4. jokes. While an album certainly doesn't have to be solemn, I encourage you not to weigh it down with jokes that are probably doomed to lose meaning over time. Humor often depends largely on awareness of contemporary, often mass, culture. Once the references are obsolete (cartoon characters, TV shows and personalities), how can anyone in the future "get it?" (For instance, I remember the 1960s icon Bobby Dylan vividly. His raspy voice is instantly recognizable to me, but not to my kids. A joke about sounding like Dylan is meaningless to them. Why include it in my album?)

Will a witty reference to a character in a Brad Pitt movie mean anything to your grandkids in 2030?

Will Madonna still be a star so that your grandchildren will chuckle at your quip under the photo of their mother, age four, in underclothes?

Some cultural icons will, of course, survive. *Jaws* or *ET*, *Jurassic Park* and *Star Wars* may be familiar to yet another generation. But since you can, why not make your album an original statement, one *in your own words*, rather than a borrowed statement from pop culture? In a photo of your son swimming towards his sister, why waste the opportunity by writing, *Here comes Jaws!* Why not write, *Matthew was always trying to surprise Amy, and she was always ready to dunk him when he came. This was how he learned to swim!* Honestly, which caption tells more about your children and which will prompt more memories when you read it in 20 years?

Strive to be a family historian not a stand-up comic in your albums.

By Hand or by Keyboard?

If you don't already have a preference about how to record your captions in your albums, you might consider these options for balancing the two goals of legibility and preserving the artifact of your handwriting (as well as giving your albums the personal touch of hand lettering).

■ **Write just the captions by hand and type your longer cameo narratives.**

■ **Do both–write everything by hand and also type at least some of your texts.** This gives the reader a choice of which to read if you combine them in one book, or gives you a text-only version to store.

■ **Write a few entries or headlines by hand and type the rest.**

Your goal is to make the stories of your life and those of your family accessible. Handwriting can be difficult to decipher - not just because of poor penmanship but because handwriting styles change and what was once easy to read can become difficult. Reading handwritten text can be tiring and unappealing. If they are illegible, your family stories may effectively be lost!

Points to Remember

EXERCISE

Go through your albums and ask yourself which captions:

1. **tell you something essential** or important about the people in the photos.

2. **do not seem to be "faded"** (i.e., as clever as when you first wrote them—now be honest with yourself!).

3. **repeat what is obvious in the images.**

Rewrite all the captions that don't meet the "test" by rewriting them using the suggestions in this chapter.

- Captions establish a **cast of characters**, a **plot** and a **setting** for your lifestory album. Captions tell your audience the **who, what, when** and **where** of your lifestory.

- Although it may be tempting to rely on borrowed phrases, *clichés*, or trendy captions as a kind of short-hand, future generations will appreciate most the captions written **in your own words.**

- Bring details into your captions—be specific by describing particular **sights, tastes, smells, sounds, textures** and **feelings**.

- You can either write your captions by hand or use a computer—there are pros and cons to both.

Chapter Five

Writing Great Cameo Narratives

The cameo narrative, after the Lifelist, is your most important photoscribing tool-whether you are creating a lifestory photo album or simply telling more of the story behind an individual photo.

Cameo narratives are longer than captions and contain more ingredients, but they remain relatively short texts-generally 50 to 150 words.

Compared to captions, cameo narratives

■ **furnish many more details.** They complete what is either not apparent or else not visible in the photo. Unlike short captions, cameos reveal much more than core information.

"When I go through my albums, it makes me happy. I really have a lovely family!"

■ **provide more space to tell your story.** The whole story is more than names, dates and locales.

■ **stand in for photos.** When no pictures are available to document an item on your Lifelist, the cameo narrative is essential to tell the story.

■ **contribute many more rich textures of feeling and life experience by adding *why* and *how*.** Life is complex and multilayered, and your albums can be, too! *Why* and *how* are often too complex to include in short captions and certainly beyond the power of a photograph to convey on its own. (If your goal is to create a lifestory photo album, you can't do it without portraying that complexity. You need cameo narratives.)

Writing Guidelines

You can help yourself to write great cameo narratives by following these steps:

1. Study your go-together photos. Place them and

your Lifelist in front of you. Group photos with items on your list and give this grouping a title. (For the time being, I'll direct you to work with cameo narratives that complement photos.)

What are you feeling or thinking as you look at the photos or read the items on your Lifelist? What comes to mind immediately? Make notes on your Lifelist of these feelings and thoughts as you experience them.

2. Write the important stuff. Ask yourself: what's crucial about this photo (these photos)? Then write what you most want people to know–facts and details you want them to remember. Trust your intuition. Often the first thought that comes to mind is the most important. Don't worry about style, grammar, or whether your writing's good enough. That's editing–a later step.

"My kids have grown up in the South. They've never had frozen mittens or seen blue shadows across a snowy field like I did as a child. I want them to get the feel of that from my album."

3. Write as short or as long a piece as you want to. If you write 20 words, your rough draft will become a caption, not a cameo narrative, but that's not a problem. Just place this text in your albums as a caption. What's important is using text to bring more meaning to your photos.

If you write 50 to 150 words, your text is called a cameo narrative. You may find that what you've written is not enough (or is too much) and you'll change the text of your cameo. Keeping yourself open to this process helps you produce the best cameo narratives you are capable of writing.

4. Keep each cameo narrative focused on one person, idea, setting, or action. If you want to write something else about that person, idea, setting, or action, draft a new cameo narrative on a separate page with its own title or heading. A story within a story can be confusing. The reader gets lost trying to follow the storyline. Let each story stand on its own.

Too much happens in one life to write it all down. Choose what tells the story best.

5. Write in short, simple sentences. Don't worry about being fancy as you put ideas into words. Simple is often best. Keeping sentences short helps you write clearly. It's not true that complicated writing has more meaning!

After a dozen words, look to end your sentence. After twenty, end it! Sentences in cameo narratives and captions should not be long and rambling.

6. Let cameo narratives be independent pieces of writing if necessary. Cameo narratives can be placed by themselves in your lifestory albums–they don't have to be connected to a photo or to another cameo narrative. They can be about a memory on your Lifelist that isn't preserved in a photo. The connection of these stand-alone cameos to your photos is an inherent one–the life you have lived.

Topics for Cameos

What sorts of topics are appropriate for you to write about in your cameo narratives? Here's a list to use to get you thinking about different possibilities:

1. Mention the reason for the photograph. Why are these people together and what impact did the event have on them? Include information about what led up to the moment pictured. This sort of cameo narrative can serve as a broad statement about your family or your life. Next to a photo of a woman in her mid-forties, this cameo narrative provides valuable info:

Paint a word picture to introduce your elders and old-time friends honestly and lovingly to your family of today and of the future.

> After the kids were grown, I was ready to work outside the home. Randall was tired after his twenty-five years at DuPont and eager for a slower pace. A job as a graphic designer fell in my lap. Randall took on the house and kept on a few accounts.

2. Depict particulars about the event or setting that are not obvious from the photo. Your cameo narratives can record details that shaped or affected the event or setting that was photographed. Include clothing, words, props, and interesting or unusual physical features.

> Nana was very proud of her mantlepiece and loved to decorate it for holidays. One year Pops ordered flowers to be delivered in time for the dinner. She was so pleased.

3. Write "portraits" of the people in the photo. There are two kinds of portraits you can include:

■ **Physical portraits.** Although the people portrayed in your albums are familiar to you, people you've loved and known, they are often unfamiliar to your children and grandchildren. Your family may not know what certain relatives looked like beyond a head shot or a picture of them in a group. Captions present names, relationships, and dates, while cameo narratives do more–they present the whole person.

> Your father's grandmother, Anya Magyar, was tall–about five foot ten–and heavy-set. Her hands and fingers were strong and broad from having worked in the fields for years. Her long, white hair was always in a bun at the back of her head. When I first met her, she looked me right in the eye and said, "Welcome to our family." She had a strong Hungarian accent.

■ **Character portraits.** Create windows on your characters' inner lives by giving your audience glimpses of how they felt, why they felt that way, and what they thought. You may have to simply tell us how you suppose your characters felt and thought–and be sure you attribute your guess work to yourself or to another person. Often guesses can be made more plausible by referring to conversations and actions of your characters.

> "Boy, that was a day!" Greg said after his first day of work at the studio. He was so full of energy; I could see he'd found something new and important. "This is it!" he said, clasping his hands. It was lovely to watch his eagerness. He'd been looking for a challenge and now he'd found one.

4. Include dialogue*. Conversations you recreate allow us to hear people's voices as you once heard them. Dialogue is so important that the entire next chapter is devoted to it.

Dialogue allows us to "hear" the voices of loved ones speaking across the years.

5. Show settings in which people lived. A setting is the environment in which your characters live and in which the action of the picture occurs. The setting includes the place (geography, buildings, interiors), the time (year, month, day, hour), and the atmosphere (mood, feeling, ethnic culture, religion, educational levels, etc.). Setting is crucial for interpreting character. It is often the most inaccessible element for your younger readers. This is unfortunate since setting is an element they will need in order to understand the story you tell in your album.

To convey setting, write portraits of houses and neighborhoods, landscapes, geographic regions, eras, seasons, and events. Culture, ethnic heritage, social, political, and even labor history can also be part of the setting for your cameo narratives.

> Our house (18 Spring St.) was three blocks from Westin School—Jamie always walked. There were so many maples on our street that in the fall, the leaves could be six inches thick on the sidewalk. The old man who lived at the corner liked having the kids stop by and made huge piles on this lawn just for them! Jamie and his pal Sam couldn't resist leaping into those leaf piles on their way to school. More than once, I got a call from the office that Jamie was late. The perfect leap into a perfect pile of leaves was just too tempting!

In describing a place, start with where the person in the picture is portrayed (in an actual or imaginary photo)

and describe everything you can see from east to west, left to right, or top to bottom. Determine an order that makes sense and follow it.

> Behind Jill is Mount James filling the horizon and Eagle Lake. It's quite shallow and fish swim close to the surface. From where she stood, you can see...

In describing a period or a culture simply write your reactions as you might in a letter or diary. (By "culture," I mean the customs and habits of a given era, region, family, generation, or institution as well as the more familiar "culture" of ethnic customs.) For instance, "In those days, people wore..." Don't presume such information is too obvious or even uninteresting to today's (and tomorrow's) audience; it paints a portrait of the time and place. If you have traveled abroad you know how fascinating the most mundane things can be-grocery packaging, for instance, in a foreign language. Your audience will be interested in the "foreign" cultures in your photos. "Why is Grandma doing that?" a child may ask, unaware that everyone did that then. (It is a recent memory for you but pre-history for your kids–so be sure to explain!)

The culture of your childhood may be as foreign to your kids or grandkids as the culture of Outer Mongolia is to you!

EXERCISE

1. Choose a photo of a person.

2. Portray that person's character by writing about some action that was typical of his or her personality.

3. Now describe the setting your character lived in. This can be your subject's community, ethnic origins, religion, or all three plus other similar kinds of setting details.

4. Combine the two–character and setting–to create one cameo narrative.

5. Now reread your cameo. Can you add more details, clarify a point, or add a sensory detail? Place the reworked piece in your *Photo Scribe Memory Binder*.

Points to Remember

- Because cameo narratives are longer than captions, they can do a better job of completing the photos and filling in the story gaps between them.
- Follow this chapter's suggested guidelines to write your cameo narratives.

■ Topics for your cameo narratives vary. Your album will be more interesting if you also vary how you write your cameo narratives.

Note to workshop leaders and teachers: The instructional worksheet, Writing Great Cameo Narratives, offers a step–by–step process for photo scribes to develop cameo narratives. Please refer to the Soleil Press Directory for info (page 119).

Chapter Six

Giving Voice To Photographs

Writing dialogue for the people who appear in your photos brings the "characters" in your lifestory photo album to life. It's important to let your children hear the voices of those who came before them. When I use the word *voice** in this context, I mean not just the sound but the whole personality and character that produced it. More than just the words spoken by someone, voice is the meaning and the significance behind those words in their life and yours. In giving voice to your characters, you will always be striving to record more than the actual words they spoke.

Habits of speech are unique characteristics that tell us about our ancestors and ourselves.

Narrative with dialogue is generally stronger and more energetic than narrative without it. For example, which of the following cameos allows us to feel Myra's presence and to hear her speaking across the years?

As a family historian, a photo scribe necessarily interprets the past as choices are made about what to write.

Cameo 1

When Myra returned from Italy, she was very excited. She had decided to take art classes at the Institute. That was the beginning of her flamboyant new "career" as an artist.

Cameo 2

"I want to paint again! Seeing those fabulous churches in Italy–it was overwhelming–the colors, the light, the marble! I just can't go back to the office and forget those paintings. Life is too short! I've decided to start at the Institute when the new term begins."

EXERCISE

1. Choose a photo of two people. Remember a conversation between them or a typical exchange. Bring their words, their tone of voice, and their habits of speech to mind.

2. Write their dialogue down.

Person 1 _____

Person 2 _____

Person 1 _____

Person 2 _____

Listen to Your Characters

Dialogue allows the reader to listen to your characters and experience them as individuals. Capture their voices on paper while they still resonate in your ears. In doing so:

■ **Make extensive use of favorite words and phrases and colloquial* sayings.**

"Dark as the inside of a pocket," Grandmother used to say.

"Two, two, two! Here me come!" Sam would call out when we played hide-and-seek.

■ **Use phonetic transcriptions*** (according to sound rather than standard spelling and grammar).

"Ain't no way, I sez ta dem, ain't no way yous guys gonna do dis!" –I can still hear Uncle Jet telling us the amazing stories from his childhood in the city. They were so exotic and remote to us farm kids on the prairie.

■ Include the pauses or other mannerisms that characterized a person's speech.

"A man and a woman…" Grandfather would say. Then he'd fall silent, looking down at his lap and his big plumber's hands. He seemed to be looking inside for the rest of his thought. It was useless to rush him or to change the topic. He'd just interrupt me in a minute to finish what he'd been saying. "… don't need to be afraid of arguing," he'd conclude. Meanwhile, I'd have drifted off into my own thoughts, and I'd wonder what he was talking about.

EXERCISE

1. Choose another photo that depicts two people.

2. For each recall any of the following as appropriate:
   ■ favorite words or expressions
   ■ accent or speech to be phonetically transcribed
   ■ notable mannerisms

3. Use these notes to put together a dialogue.

Person 1 _____

Person 2 _____

Person 1 _____

Person 2 _____

Person 1 _____

Person 2 _____

How to Use Dialogue

You can use dialogue in your cameo narratives to record:

1. what people were saying to each other at the time of the photo or around that time.

"You coming to the corn roast tonight?" Jayne wanted to know.

"Will there be dessert?" I asked. Of all my cousins, she was the one I could tease the most. I still miss that banter and it's ten years now since she moved away. "Not unless you get busy in this kitchen!" she shot back.

2. a typical conversation even if it was not spoken on the very occasion of a specific photo.

"What do you want to do?" my father used to ask me. "What sort of job do you think you'd be happy at?"

"I don't know," I'd answer.

"So what would you be good at?" he'd ask, trying again. And I still didn't know.

3. an individual's response to the photo many years later. A third-person comment offers a glimpse into two characters, the speaker and her subject.

"Laura had many talents," her mother said to me at her daughter's funeral. "Did you ever hear her sing? Oh my! what a strong voice. I'd always have goose bumps when her voice filled the hall at Convocation!"

Using Foreign Words

Foreign words are fine–go ahead and use them. (It's easy to check that you are preserving correct spellings by using on-line dictionaries.)

Of course, unless your family is still fluent in the language, it's awkward to use it extensively. But a few well-chosen words and phrases, especially when they are part of your memories, add interest without being difficult to understand. Words and phrases like *Mother, Father, I love you,* or the names of special foods or clothing in an original language are an

"Mon petit chou, my grandmother called us. Nobody's called me 'my little cabbage' since!"

affirmation of your family identity.

There are ways to make another language accessible in your album.

■ **Put a translation in parenthesis immediately after the non-English word**-"*plaçek* (a sweet Polish bread)."

■ **Paraphrase the word or phrase right away**-"*Te quiero*," she said. "I love you." (This is the method I prefer because it leaves no doubt.)

Note that whenever you use a non-English word, it is *italicized*, or underlined if you are writing by hand. (Some words have been adopted into English and no longer need to be, but can be, italicized: you can write either "cliche" or "*cliché*.")

Direct and Indirect Dialogue

While dialogue can make your writing come to life, not all dialogue is equally effective.

There are two kinds of dialogue: direct and indirect.

■ **Direct dialogue is a straight quote.** The words a person spoke, or is alleged to have spoken, are used. Begin and end a direct quote with quotation marks. The tags *he said* and *she said* are placed outside of the quotation marks. Sentence punctuation goes inside the quotes.

Mama said, "I made my best blueberry pie ever just for you!"

Most of the time, it's best not to get fancy with dialogue tags. Using tags like "she chortled" and "he riposted" can get out of hand quickly! Simplicity is always best. It's the quote, after all, not the tag, that you want to make memorable.

■ **Indirect dialogue is an allusion to speech.** It is introduced by "that." Indirect dialogue is an approximation, not necessarily the actual words. Indirect dialogue doesn't usually use quotation marks but sometimes does. (Quotation marks indicate that the speaker used those specific words.) Here are two ways to write indirect dialogue:

> Mama said that she had made her best blueberry pie ever just for us.

> Mama said that she had made her "best blueberry pie ever" just for us.

In the last example, the phrase "best blueberry pie ever" is what Mama actually said; the rest is approximation. The quotation marks signal the reader that you have approximated what's not within them.

Direct dialogue makes a stronger statement than indirect dialogue. Test this by re-reading the examples above. The *direct* dialogue is more immediate; the *indirect* is less so because the speaker is heard through an approximation.

Although indirect dialogue has less impact, it is nonetheless an effective tool when you are uncomfortable or unable to attribute words directly.

> I remember Barb saying that we *shouldn't* bring the issue up to the group and Nancy insisting that we *should* talk about it with the others before it was too late.

Clearly, this lacks the drama of:

> "Don't you ever raise that topic in the group," said Barb. "It's inappropriate and totally uncalled for!"

> "We should get it out in the open!" countered Nancy. "We'll regret it if we don't!"

Tips for Writing Dialogue

1. You'll often need to make up dialogue–whether direct or indirect. Is this okay? Well, it's inevitable. You didn't have a tape recorder to get the exact words. You are remembering what your character *likely* spoke aloud. So you approximate. Most dialogues in your album will be approximations. That's a good reason to keep them short. They are more likely to be authentic and less likely to be inaccurate that way. One day, you may be surprised to overhear another generation repeating your approximation as a "truth!" That's why it's so important to photoscribe your albums thoughtfully. Regardless of what *really* happened, your version of it, preserved in your album and read and re-read over the years, will become the "truth" as it is known from now on.

Children come up with some great phrases when they use new language skills to describe their discoveries in the world! Keep a notebook for writing them down right away.

2. Make your quotes sound like that person's voice. Ask that person if your quote is right, or close your eyes and imagine them speaking to you. Listen with your inner ear. If you feel uncomfortable with what you write, take it as a sign that the dialogue is "off."

3. Dialogue works best when limited to two to four exchanges. Often, a single exchange is enough. (One speaks, another answers.) You can also simply report what one person said without any response.

4. Dialogue can be included in several ways in a cameo narrative.

■ It can be most of the cameo narrative or all of it.

"Your Aunt Lee had music in her bones," Gran said. "That's her with the violin. Grandpa bought it from the music teacher. She took lessons for years. She'd always be asked to play when the family got together. And she started playing for weddings when she was just 15. Oh, she was *good!*" Her eyes would close, and I knew she was hearing Aunt Lee play and feeling pride in her again.

■ **More than one dialogue can be placed in a single cameo narrative.** They should focus, however, on the same person, place, or thing (in this case, Aunt Lee's musical gift).

"Lee was my musical one," Gran said, "always 'playing music' on barrels in the barn or even on my pots and pans before Grandpa bought the fiddle."

"When she got to high school," my father once told me, Lee's music teacher told Gran and Grandpa, 'This girl has got to go to the Conservatory.' She got a lot of attention for that."

■ **Dialogue can be placed within a setting, a character portrait, or any other text.**

"Your aunt was a musical child," Gran said, looking at her gallery of family photos on the wall. They were all there: her parents, my grandfather, Gran's second husband (Mr. Al), her children (Mom and my aunts and uncles), my siblings, and all of her other grandchildren.

Points to Remember

■ Dialogue is what people say. It adds variety and energy to your writing.

■ Dialogue expresses individual personality and character. It brings your characters to life.

■ Direct dialogue is a straight quote; indirect dialogue alludes to speech and isn't always written in quotation marks.

■ Dialogue can stand alone or be part of a larger piece.

Chapter Seven

Using Action & Other Suggestions

By varying what you write in your cameo narratives, you make your albums more interesting to read.

1. Use action-based cameo narratives to make your albums less static.

> The hill was long and well-iced. At night, the floodlights were on, but there were deep shadows at the edge. The children ran hard from the wall to the crest of the hill and then jumped on the toboggan. They'd cling to each other, legs in the air. Someone would always fall off halfway down or they'd run into other sledders or hit the ski jump. Screaming, they'd tumble off in front of another sled, barely missing the stream at the bottom of the run.

■ **The action you choose for a cameo narrative doesn't need to be dramatic.** (Life's quiet moments make good cameo narratives, too.) Here's an example of quiet drama:

> Every day for ten years, I drove Route 9 to work. From several points on that road in the winter and early spring, I would see the White Mountains, especially the peak of Mount Washington, a hundred and twenty miles away.

■ **Don't be reluctant to write about more momentous, life-changing events.** It is not in bad taste to write about tragic occurrences. Keep in mind to write simply and clearly, especially when dealing with difficult events.

In this same '74 VW bus, Belinda and Jim drove to the west coast in 1978. The accident was two years later. They were coming home from the city and there was freezing rain that night. Jim hit a slick spot on the curve and lost control. They plunged down the cliff at Ocean Drive right onto those massive granite rocks where we used to climb as children. Belinda and Jim died that day: March 7, 1980.

■ **Show your story, don't tell it.** I can't overemphasize this! The reader must "see" your characters in actions that reveal their personalities and temperaments. Don't just tell how nurturing your father was. Show him in the action of nurturing someone.

Imagine that, instead of writing, you are using a movie camera to tell your story. Movie cameras can only capture tangible details. They don't *tell* us that people are happy. They show us people being happy, doing happy things. With the movie camera model in mind, write the action itself. Don't write, *I was happy.* Write, *When Martin got the promotion, we kept catching each other suddenly smiling! All the tension of the last two years was gone.*

Writing a vivid and colorful word picture is the secret to really effective photoscribing.

In the following narratives, note which **tells** that the mother was kind and which **shows** us how she was. Which cameo will your family will find more interesting and more convincing of your mother's kindness?

Cameo 1

Mother was always very kind to my high school friend, Tara, whose mother died when she was 14. One year she took her shopping for a winter coat.

Cameo 2

Mom noticed my friend Tara shivering as she waited for me in front of the school. "Where's your winter coat?"

"It doesn't fit," Tara answered. "Dad's working overtime. I don't know when he can take me shopping."

"Well," said Mother looking at me pointedly. "Renée and I are going on Saturday. Why don't you come, too?" It was the first I'd heard that we were going shopping. That was my mother—she saw the need and just took care of it.

EXERCISE

1. Make a short list of people (2 or 3) in your life.

2. Brainstorm adjectives that describe each individual (e.g., beautiful, smart, kind).

3. Now, using the five senses, specifically show the meaning of the adjective. For instance, replace "kind" with a specific action (she *put her arm around Amy and gave her a hug*) that *shows* her being kind.

4. Now write the stories which show the context of the adjectives you chose above. Include specific details (i.e., who was there, what was happening, etc.).

---

2. Include the best features of captions in your cameos. These are precise dates, full names of people and places, and references to relationships. Or, write both a caption with these details and a cameo narrative that is full of action, dialogue, setting, etc.

3. Avoid abstract words and phrases in your writing. This is a close cousin to **show, don't tell.** When words and phrases are vague, they conjure different images for different people. Although the reader always brings her own interpretation and experience to your writing, your specific words and phrases will guide her to understand and accept your point of view as abstract ones cannot.

When a college friend once said, "We were poor when I was young," the power of images to convey meaning grew very clear as she added without a trace of irony, "Our maid left every night after dinner. I was the only one of my high-school friends who didn't have a live-in maid!"

Enable your reader to "see" everything you write–your characters, settings, and actions–by using specific and striking details. These are more likely to mean the same thing to different people. Writing in images will help you convey your meaning. Instead of writing *She was a pretty woman*, write what she looked like *(auburn hair, 5 foot 4 inches, fit and slender)*, what she wore *(earth-colored corduroy jumpers)* and what her bearing was *(strode quickly)*. Instead of *It was a big downtown*, describe the size of the stores, their color, shape, and construction *(square, three-storey, wood-frame buildings)*. What specific features of climate or vegetation were typical *(sugar maples* and not *trees)* and what were the winters like *(10 below* and not *cold, 18 inches of snow* and not *lots of snow)*. Describe action with details, too.

On late winter days, I'd get my snowshoes and put Zoé on my back. As I pulled the toboggan of sap buckets across the thinning snow, Zoé would jump up and down in the backpack, excited by the crisp air and bright sun that cast lengthening shadows across the field. "Zoé warm enough? You like the snow?" I'd ask her. In the woods, we'd visit every maple. Zoé would lean way over to watch, tipping my balance as I poured the jugs of sap into buckets. Gradually, heading back across the field, I'd feel her slump as she fell asleep. That was the first of many years of maple sapping with my children. The next year, Max was on my back, and Zoé was bundled up in the sled. March became a favorite time of year for me and for them. Maple time.

■ **Be precise in your observations.** Don't make use of general phrases like *majestic mountain*. If the mountain is granite and has two peaks, write *twin, granite-capped peaks*. If the mountain is completely forested with pines, write *covered with pointed pines*.

4. Be sure to write about what is not photographed

as well as what is. A lifestory photo album is based on the Lifelist, not merely on the photos you happen to have on hand. Work with the storyline of your Lifelist to become familiar with the gaps where life was lived but not photographed. These are perfect opportunities for cameo narratives.

EXERCISE

Free Writing

1. Write a cameo narrative for an event for which you have no photograph.
■ **Include facts** (names, actions, addresses), **feelings** ("I felt so hopeful then"), *and* **impressions** ("warmest day," "proud of her hat"). Without paying attention to style or grammar, write a journal entry for each topic or memory.

2. For each different memory, use a new page. Keeping one memory per page will help you to organize later. Concentrate on getting words on paper.

3. Use this free writing as source material. Having lots of notes is helpful when you combine or refine it later as you rewrite.

5. Include life's ordinary moments in your cameo narratives. Give yourself the assignment to write about a typical, not special, day or activity. Where are the photos of you in the first hours of the day, at work where you spend so much of your life, or doing mundane tasks like laundry, dishes, driving, phone calls? Cameo narratives *"My favorite moments of the day are early mornings when I'm the first one up having a cup of coffee on the deck."* can capture memories worth preserving that may not make good photos. Paint a word picture instead.

6. Make lists—include parts of your Lifelist that you don't want to develop into stories of their own. In

Chapter 2, I suggest that Lifelist notes should be brief–often no more than three to five words. You can include Lifelist items "as is" in your album, or you may want to add text to make them meaningful. For instance, "barn cats" might become "on the farm, there were always half-wild cats that never came in the house." As you view the Lifelist, what will you need to add to make every item on the list meaningful? Write briefly but in sufficient detail to ensure the memory, however small, will be preserved and stand on its own.

Art Club Harvest Dinner

Menu: *Mushroom rissoles, roasted vegetables, sage stuffing, oignons dorés, pecan pie, coffee.* **Guests:** *Will and Judith, Kathleen, Ed, Jean, Sarah and Vincent, Steven and Peter, Moira.* **Decorations:** *waxed leaves and ribbons, berries with dried flowers, Jean's shadow lights; gold, sienna, loden green linens.*

List names of people, places, and favorite things. For example, to accompany a photo of you at thirteen, you might add a list titled *My favorite songs in seventh grade.*

Recipes, menus, poems, prayers, songs, or sayings can also stand alone as cameo narratives, sharing more of the whole of your complex life which your photos depict.

7. Include maps, house and floor plans, drawings, tickets, programs–anything you want. Plan ahead to include all these elements: photos, text, and artifacts. Be sure to include cameo narratives to accompany artifacts as well as photographs.

8. Musings* make effective cameo narratives. Musings (*I've always wondered...*or *What if...*) record your longings and reveal your imaginative life. Though a journal may be a more useful place for open-ended exploration of life choices, choosing to photoscribe important or characteristic musings adds a deeper, more personal level to your albums. This category may appeal more to older photo scribes who are looking back over a lifetime and evaluating decisions and events.

EXERCISE

1. Write a Limited Lifelist that details your daily activities. If you have young children, you may be in that era when you can't believe you will ever be doing anything but changing diapers and picking up toys. But sooner than you think, your daily routines will be entirely different. Start today to do a Limited Lifelist of whatever occupies your days.

2. Use this list to generate both cameo narratives and photos of the ordinary moments you will cherish years from now. How about a word picture of getting the kids dressed to go out to play?

3. Place your Limited Lifelist directly in your album or record your musings about that activity or time in your life.

Points to Remember

- Using action in your cameo narratives will add variety to your album.
- Show, don't tell. Let specific details convey your meaning. Abstract words and phrases mean different things to different people.
- Cameo narratives can vary widely in their content.

Chapter Eight

Stage By Stage : A Writing Primer

Being aware of the three different stages of writing, and their respective challenges and opportunities, will make you a more effective photo scribe.

The stages are **writing the rough draft*, rewriting*** for more meaning and more precise meaning, and **editing*** the final copy. Each stage is important in creating a lifestory album and is creative and rewarding in its own way. In the exercises you have completed already, you have worked parts of each of these stages. In this chapter, you study them all together.

Stage One : The Rough Draft

The first stage of photoscribing is to write a rough draft. This is the raw material from which the final, polished cameo will be crafted.

I know that some people approach writing as a horrible, difficult task. Putting words down on paper is anxious and unpleasant for them. If you are

"I like being able to call it a 'rough' draft—it frees me from having to be my perfect self all the time!"

new to the expressive writing of photoscribing or reluctant because of past lack of success, consider this: writing is like cooking!

You need a well-tested recipe (provided by this book), the raw ingredients (your life experiences and your photos assembled in a rough draft like so many vegetables and seasonings), and the willingness and time to do each step one after the other.

Nobody's asking you to make a gourmet banquet for sixty! Begin to build your skills and your confidence with simple projects. If writing doesn't come easily to you, don't get discouraged. It will get easier with practice.

Write each rough draft on a separate piece of paper to make the later stage of rewriting easier.

There's no better way to learn to write than to write regularly. Just start putting down what comes to mind. Don't wait for just the right word or feeling. If you have jotted something dull on paper, you can rewrite it more interestingly later, but you can't rewrite anything unless you've got a rough draft to work with!

Rough Draft Samples

Here are four rough drafts that tell four stories. I wrote the memories down just as they came to me while I lingered with this picture.

Cameo 1

My Ledoux grandparents always sat in different rooms, not like my other grandparents who were inseparable and always chatted with each other about anything and everything. I didn't think anything of this at the time. As an adult, I can see that perhaps they weren't well-matched. Maybe my grandmother was lonely in her marriage. She didn't get to show her playful side too much. My grandfather wanted order and regularity, but I wonder if he was lonely, too.

Cameo 2

My grandmother Ledoux lived upstairs from us. She always played favorites. I know her choices were sometimes fickle. I happened to be one of her favorites because she felt that she and I shared similar interests and similar spirits. I appreciated something in her that *Pépère* and Dad and Mom didn't.

Cameo 3

My grandmother Ledoux was, it seems to me, a woman who believed she couldn't have a good relationship with sons but had to focus on her daughter. Unfortunately, her only daughter moved 3,000 miles away to California! *Mémère* was given to bouts of melancholia. Her relationship with *Pépère*—who was a silent and introverted man—didn't give her much relief. Two of her children lived near her, but they were sons and I don't think she could open herself to men.

Cameo 4

My grandmother Ledoux had a much lighter sense of herself and of life than *Pépère* did. He craved order and regularity; she craved disorder and spontaneity. They didn't resolve this difference over the years. There was always a tension between them about it. Although she's indulging her lighter side in this picture and he is uncharacteristically submitting to it good-naturedly enough, this is not what I remember as typical.

In writing a rough draft, I let my imagination and my memory-rather than the photograph or my album-be my guide.

In the rough draft stage, don't worry about whether the writing is meaningful or polished. Your goal is to get words on paper. I set rough draft narratives aside in my *Photo Scribe Memory Binder* (see Soleil Press Directory, page 119) until I'm ready to work on them again. That comes after I've lingered with both photos and stories long enough to feel that I am telling the story I want to tell. Referring to my Lifelist helps me be sure not to omit an obvious link or another memory. Only when I'm confident my story is whole do I place the photos and final cameo permanently in my album. (See Chapter 9, "Putting It All Together.")

Don't be discouraged when you see the need for change. Most writing can be improved at every stage.

I have choices about how to use these cameos. They can be linked as one long piece. Or, I can keep them as short pieces interspersed throughout the pages that feature my grandparents. After all, each tells a different story about them and about my experience of them. Even if I use only one and discard the others, I have focused my memory on two important people in my life. Writing freely reacquaints me with feelings and facts that inform my choice of what to include in the final draft. (See page 86, "Rewriting Sample.")

Some photoscribes find that rewriting is the most creative part of writing.

Writing the rough draft almost always points you in the proper direction. Writing uncritically at this early stage provides you with the most raw ingredients to work with later.

EXERCISE

1. Choose several photos that are important to you. They should be pictures you'd like to learn more about.

2. Write at least three rough drafts of a cameo narrative for each photograph. Write about a different aspect of the photo in each draft. Use dialogue, action, setting, and character. Include sensory details to make your story come alive.

3. Review what you have written. What do you want to share and what do you want to keep private? Which of the rough drafts will you develop into finished cameo narratives?

Stage Two: Rewriting

Rewriting is the second stage of photoscribing. It's not a matter of just changing *these* words for *those*. It's a separate and essential stage of the writing process. Rewriting is your opportunity to communicate what you really mean.

Rewriting is fine-tuning. Ask yourself, "Is there anything I'm leaving out because I might not yet be aware of it, because I don't know how to say it, or because I don't dare to say it?"

To answer these questions:

■ **Look inward** in order to identify what you want and need to say.

■ **Review your Lifelist** and linger with your photos to extract the most memory you can from them.

■ **Choose potent words and phrases** which will communicate the most meaning. Discard those worn-out, flavorless words like nice and good.

There are so many good ways to tell a story that you don't need to worry much about finding the one right way!

At this stage, make sure you do these three things:

1. Double-check basic facts and relationships ascribed to your photos. Have you included the appropriate and accurate information: the *who, what, where, when, how,* and *why?* Are you sure–absolutely–about what you say you remember and the consequences of it? (We frequently make inferences from what we know. Unfortunately, we aren't always accurate.) Memories, as we've seen, can trick us. Is it the event or a memory of the event you are remember-

ing? Perhaps your cross-check or research will lead you to rewrite in order to give new information. Or you may decide to note that you are recording your version which hasn't been, or can't be, verified.

2. Focus each cameo narrative on only one character, action, or setting. Create a narrative that makes a focused statement.

> Jan spent that winter sorting out her things. She kept saying, 'Simplify, simplify," as she carted boxes to Goodwill.

When you mix more than one focus in a single cameo, your writing loses its impact.

> Tony was a great gardener and he had a kayak.

The preceding example makes two statements. You can refocus the text around a single statement. Here's a rewrite that uses a new introductory sentence to bring the two parts of the cameo together in one unified statement.

> Tony always loved to be outdoors. He grew a large vegetable garden and took his kayak out on the river whenever he could.

Or, you can place the second statement *(he had a kayak)* with another photo and let it be its own cameo.

3. Blend character, action, setting, dialogue, and style in your cameo narratives. This full mix of writing elements adds variety and makes your cameo narratives

more interesting and informative. These impart to your writing "soup" a richer flavor and entice your audience to read on. (Remember, as in #2 above, that your cameo must have one focus.)

The following cameo is a rewrite of the short cameo above. Notice how much richer it has become due to the diversity of elements added during the rewriting stage.

> Tony was an outdoors type. I can see him now, hauling hay to mulch his garden, forking great clumps of soil to prepare the beds. "I'd love to spend some time with you," he'd say. "Why don't you come out to visit on Saturday?" And he'd grin hopefully, knowing I'd rather visit over cappuccino in town. "Coming out to visit" meant several hours of weeding and a death-defying kayak trip on the river as a treat.

4. Use the five senses in captions and cameo narratives to show rather than tell.

Sensory details give your writing immediacy. Use specific sensations–taste, smell, sound, the color, texture, shape, and feel of objects–so your reader experiences them. Avoid the abstract (*a lovely smell*) in favor of the tangible (*the sharp scent of wet pine needles*).

In both short captions and cameo narratives, show rather than tell by using specific and striking details.

EXERCISE

1. Review at least five cameo narratives you have already written. (By now, you have many on hand!)

2. Rewrite each following the guidelines mentioned above. Which points are the most difficult for you to adapt? Which are the easiest? Why?

3. Study differences between your rough drafts and rewrites. Do the rewrites have the best parts of the roughs?

The Rewriting Process

You can be more effective in rewriting your cameo narratives if you pay attention not only to *what* your text says but *how* it says it. Be willing to rework your writing. Why should it be perfect on the first try?

1. Put your rough draft aside. Time–two days, a week, or even a month–will make you more objective and better able to assess what your writing does and doesn't say.

2. Role-play reading your text with fresh, observant eyes and critical ears. Imagine you are a stranger who does not know you nor has any attachment to your text. This person might say, "Let's see. Some cameo narratives by So-and-So. Are they any good?" Read from that imaginary person's perspective. Does your text seem interesting and meaningful? If not, make the necessary changes to correct the criticisms.

3. Show your writing to others for critique. Family feedback can be useful to add or corroborate information and details. On the other hand, friends who don't already know (and haven't lived through) your stories can alert you about where they lose the thread or don't "get it."

When choosing a person to ask to help you in this process, be wary of the following:

■ **People who make only supportive comments.** "Isn't that nice, dear. I like anything you do!"

■ **People who call their version of the story right and yours all wrong.**

You can, however, always learn something from feedback. A disagreement with a spouse or a relative may make you realize that the same story has more than one side and you should provide multiple versions for accuracy. In this case, write, *According to John, the kids at that age were…, but in my experience…*

Let others organize their own photoscribed lifestory albums if they have some-thing different to say!

Friends and colleagues will provide valuable perspectives different from your relatives' because they aren't under the influence of family rules and assumptions. They may tell you, "I don't understand why your sister did this. It seems out of character for the woman you describe in this other cameo narrative." Your reader might ask, "Why did your husband say that? It's not clear to me why you interpret it as supportive of you. He comes across as very cold."

We are all given (or trained) to take the peculiarities of our own families for granted. New photo scribes may find they are simply repeating hand-me-down versions of a family story. It's important personal work to discover the true story "according to you."

4. Eliminate *clichés* and stereotypes. Check both captions and cameo narratives for *clichés (a spry 76-years-young)*, stereotypes *(men don't know a thing about kids!)*, stale, cute phrases *(it's a girl thing!)*. Trade these *clichés* and stereotypes for phrases that convey real information based on specific and accurate details of setting, character, or action. (If these categories don't resonate for you, substitute your ethnic, religious or racial group so you get the point.) Stereotypes are not only weak writing, they separate us from understanding.

Some people hoard words and phrases—they can't bear to throw any away!

Replace trendy phrases because they say little now and will mean even less in twenty years. (Consider the once popular 1920's expression "twenty-three skiddoo!" Now what does *that* mean?!)

5. Rework your text if you have to explain to make a point clear. Since you won't always be there to clarify, make your cameo narratives–either singly or in groups–so articulate that readers will understand without extra help.

If you find you have to explain further, add what you say to your written text, or replace what you've written with what you're saying out loud to complete the story.

6. Find a friend and be a friend. Writing buddies can be very helpful as you write and rewrite. Friends can not only tell you if your cameo narratives leave them wanting more or are unclear, they can also give you encouragement.

If it stimulates your creativity to share the design and production phases with fellow scrapbookers, you'll enjoy writing together, too. The companionship of a fellow photo scribe is rewarding and can be crucial to your perseverance.

Rewriting Sample

Remember the cameo narrative drafts I wrote for the photos on page 78 and 79? Here's my rewrite:

Walking in on my Ledoux grandparents in their upstairs apartment in the house we shared on the Ridge, I'd always find them sitting in different rooms. They wouldn't be chatting together like my other grandparents. While their silence didn't seem to bother *Pépère*, it did grate on my grandmother. *Mémère* was given to bouts of moodiness that her relationship with *Pépère—a* silent and introverted man—didn't help. As an adult, I wonder what it was about their relationship that didn't permit them to help each other more?

It's interesting to me that *Pépère* is so good-naturedly submitting to her teasing. He was usually more serious and he craved order and regularity. It's not a typical scene of them at all, not one that I remember. She must have been lonely. She didn't often show this playful, humorous side of herself.

Because I am a writer, my choice is usually to include more text rather than less in an album. You might choose differently. That's ok. Just make sure that your choices convey as much of the story as you can tell, especially when you are recording family history for another generation.

Stage Three: Editing Techniques

Rewriting and editing are not entirely distinct activities. As you rewrite, you will also edit, and while you edit you will do some rewriting. But there is a key difference. As you rewrite, you generally continue to produce text. **Rewriting is usually an expanding process.** As you edit, however, your task is not to add more words. Instead, you are polishing the text that exists. **Editing is therefore often (but not always) usually a contracting process.**

There are points to keep in mind when you edit.

1. Check spelling, grammar, and punctuation. These really aren't monsters created to make your life miserable. Think of them as tools to allow you to communicate effectively with your readers. By following conventions of spelling, grammar, and punctuation you make it easy for others to understand your text.

2. Verify spellings for every name and foreign word you use. Think of Ellis Island–and the names that were changed forever. Your spellings may be the documentation future generations use. Be sure you're not setting a false standard for them.

3. Examine your vocabulary to make sure you have used words your family can understand and identify with. Resist the urge to reach for a fancy *Remember: you're not just archiving photographs, you're recording a lifestory for posterity.* turn of phrase. Better to write simple sentences and be proud of them than to sound foolish in an attempt to impress! *Simple,* however, doesn't mean exhausted words like *nice* and *good.* Make every word carry its own weight of meaning.

4. Reread for consistency. Consistency is a term which is broader than the term *focus* in its application. **Consistency means that each element in your narrative is in keeping with every other.** Your narrative, of course, needs to be focused on one character, action, or setting. It needs something more, however. Its vocabulary, type of sentence structure, point of view, and tone all need to be consistent throughout. Consistency has to do with the style and the mechanics of your prose.

5. Check your writing for coherence. Your story must make sense, and not wander off this way and that way. Coherence has to do with the ideas. They have to hang together and be clear as to what they mean. When someone says your writing is rambling, they most likely mean that it is not coherent. Clarity is a another word that is sometimes used to mean coherence.

6. Make your writing concise. Use as few words as you need, to say just what you want to say. Eliminate redundancies, material that does not contribute directly to the overall impact of your captions or cameos. Being concise is always helped by the application of the ten-percent rule: cross out one word in every ten in your text. Most writing can be improved by making it shorter and more to the point.

Working on many cameo narratives at once can be an effective method.

Points to Remember

- There are three stages to photoscribing: creating rough drafts, rewriting, and editing.
- The rough draft is the raw material out of which you craft your writing.
- Rewriting is an opportunity to communicate what you really want to say.
- Editing is a stage of getting your language in line with conventions for the sake of clear communication.

Chapter Nine

Putting It All Together

The time has come to put your captions, cameos, photos, and artifacts together in your lifestory photo album. **The life you and your family have lived, and not the photos you have, is at the core of the story this album must tell.** Of course, the photos you have on hand form a visual focus, but what you see is never the whole nor the limit of your story.

In creating lifestory photo albums, you may find, as I have, that you have clusters of photos around a single event-one Christmas when the camera was new and the photographer was very enthusiastic. However, you may have no photo to document another time you remember well and which was perhaps more significant-the winter when your father fell sick and died, for instance.

"Now it's all gone except for the memories... I've never forgotten those people–though with every passing year the voices grow dimmer."
—Woody Allen, in "Radio Days"

That is why cameo narratives are so important. They tell the stories behind your photos, but they can also tell the stories for which there are no photos.

Art gallery and museum directors will tell you how important it is to hang a show well. "Well" means arranging pieces in the best relationships to each other and to the white space around them on the wall. A properly-displayed show emphasizes the artist's vision while a poorly-displayed one obscures or, at best, ignores it.

The same is true for your albums. Ones with well-grouped photos and cameo narratives will tell your story much more thoroughly and effectively than those in which photos and text are poorly arranged.

Many Photos

If you have many photos, you can be selective in which ones you keep. Since the mid-sixties, we've taken multiple pictures of not just one event but of one pose or scene. The technology–especially now that it's digital–is so easy we can produce too many photos.

You could photoscribe and scrapbook every one of your photos, but the cost in time and supplies may be prohibitive.

1. Select a smaller number of photos for your lifestory photo album.

Look at all these photos of his car! I'd give anything to have a picture of Brian instead. It was the last time he came.

■ **Choose the best photos.** Look for subject, focus, print quality, composition (how subjects are positioned in relation to each other and the background).

■ **Choose photos that tell a story beyond the immediate subject.** Look for plenty of details in the background. Don't automatically discard pictures that are not of the best photographic quality. In two photos of family members at a reunion, for instance, one may give a clear background view of a piece of furniture you remember or of a favorite aunt. Use this background piece or person as a stimulus for a cameo narrative and to tell a story that is not evident in the photo.

■ **When you crop photos, don't throw out anything essential in the image.** Pay attention to artifacts in the background that tell the story of your family or ethnic group. Decorations or objects familiar in your own childhood may be obscure but important clues when your children start exploring their heritage.

Cropping can be compared to the 1950's craze of cutting the elaborate headboards off Victorian beds to create a "modern" look. How wonderful it would be if our parents and grandparents had not "modernized" in this way and had left those old-fashioned beds intact! Don't give your kids reasons to say the same about enthusiastic photo cropping!

■ **Favor photos generated by important moments rather than by random and artificial "photo opportunities."** It's so easy to take photos today! We've all taken them of moments that are not (when all is said and done) particularly significant–or even interesting to us. These are not the shots of life's ordinary moments (you at the library checking a book out) which can provide a meaningful story for the future. What I'm calling "photo opportunities" are those poses that essentially connect neither to ordinary moments nor to meaningful ones. For instance, does a photo of Jason in a sombrero (which your husband Matt plopped on his head as you were leaving a Mexican restaurant at the mall) preserve any real information about your son or your family? Does it evoke a significant memory with associations and family history attached? Not unless you once lived in Mexico or shows him in a typical mood.

Honor how much effort you're investing in photoscribing meaningful albums by working with your most significant images.

2. Select the primary photos to include in your albums. Take one or more of the following steps to preserve and make use of the extras:

■ **Label them clearly** with a photo-safe pencil.

■ **Write info on Post-it notes** for safe temporary identification.

■ **Store them in an archival envelope** noting subject, time, and the album where similar photos can be found.

■ **Trade them with relatives.**

■ **Keep them for your children.**

■ **Use them in a second album** for a relative or friend. A lifestory photo album makes a wonderful gift.

Few Photos

Before the mid-sixties, people took many fewer photos than they do now. A lifestory photo album requires that you not only tell the story behind your photos but that you tell the story of the missing photos, too.

1. When you have too few photos, cameo narratives can bridge the gaps in your story. Compare your Lifelist to the photos you have in your collection and other pictures you have access to. Wherever you have gaps, record the experience in a cameo narrative. These gaps may occur in any album but are more prevalent in a heritage album that seeks to tell lifestories from the past.

2. Artifacts can fill out or complete an album. These include post cards, newspaper clippings that portray some phase of your life, or of the life of your subject.

In an album dedicated to your father who was a firefighter, why not include reproductions of historic photos of his fire station, tickets to the firemen's ball, an antique post card of the fire station, or a photocopy of an article from the local newspaper's archives–especially one in which he or his unit is mentioned.

For another page, you might include a recipe or the verses of a hymn, the map of a town or the floor plan of the house where you grew up. Include tickets and ribbons, etc. It's your album. Just put as much care into selecting and preserving your memorabilia as you do your photos. Use cameo narratives to make clear links between your artifacts, your photos, and the storyline they convey.

"Heaven and earth shall pass away, but my words shall not pass away."
—Matthew 24:35

An institution that has played a role in the life of the person who is your subject is also a good focus for a mixed-media album with photos, artifacts, and cameos.

3. Today's photos of your life's important buildings and places can help you to document the past. Go to places that were important to you or to the person whose story you are telling. Photograph the house, for instance, where your parents lived when you were born. If you are aware of changes to the house, you can write, for instance, *The picture window in front was a later addition, replacing two small windows.*

4. Photo-editing technology now makes it possible to make new images from old. Not only can you repair damaged photos you can create new ones!

■ **You can add or remove people and elements from photos.** For instance, you have no photos of your mother and her three sisters together. With computer programs now widely available, you can group people from different photos into a new composite image! (This is why photographs are no longer allowed as evidence in court.) You can eliminate elements, too. Of course, when you alter images, you have a responsibility to let your audience know. To do otherwise is falsifying a record—and creating a lie.

The explanation itself can be an important addition to your family story!

> I removed my father's cousin from this photo. Mom and Dad borrowed money from him to buy their house on Ocean Street. He foreclosed on the loan when Dad was injured at work. Then he turned around and sold the house for a big profit. I couldn't bring myself to include him in this album.

■ **You can improve elements in your pictures.** You can change colors, eliminate obtrusive backgrounds, lighten dark areas, bring a face out of the shadows, or eliminate stains and creases.

Print your altered photos (or get them printed) on photo-safe paper on a high resolution printer. All these services are available in home computer software or by working with a professional. Look in the Yellow Pages under *Photo Retouching and Restoration* for specialists near you.

Organizing Your Lifestory Photo Albums

1. Use the following suggestions as organizing principles for placing your cameo narratives and photos in an album:

■ **Chronology**

Most photo scribes choose to organize their albums by time. Arrange your photos and texts in the same sequence as the events they portray or describe. Childhood, youth, middle-age, then retirement; spring, summer, fall, then winter. Chronology always offers a natural progression for an album.

■ **Theme**

You may want to organize some or all of your albums around specific topics or events. A theme album can feature photos and cameo narratives that celebrate career, marriage, vacations, or a new home. A theme album's internal organization is often chronological.

■ Character (Biography)

You can focus your album on one person's life. Such commemorative albums are especially cherished at times of celebrations or of loss. Mother's Day, Father's Day, graduation, the death of an individual. When biography is your main focus, you also have the choice to develop your albums with an internal organization by chronology (birth to present day) or theme (career, for instance).

■ All of the above

Although you may begin to photoscribe your lifestory albums using one of these organizing principles, you will likely find yourself combining them. There is no one correct way. You may want to interrupt the chronological order of several albums to create a theme album for the birth of a child, the story of a house being built, or a special celebration.

2. The Lifelist remains the inner core of your albums' organization. However you conceive of your photo albums, always refer to your Lifelist for cues about how to organize your albums.

Placing Narratives in Your Albums

Where do you place your cameo narratives in the pages of your photo albums? Here are some suggestions:

1. When you have more photos than cameo narratives, place cameos on the page as you do photos. Using the layouts you have perfected, create attractive pages in which both the photos and the text serve as design blocks.

Both the text and the photos will be enhanced by color backgrounds, borders or other design elements such as cut-outs or decals. Your choice of period-appropriate colors and headline fonts can enhance the stories you are telling.

Don't let your page design overpower the readability of the text.

2. When you have more cameo narratives than photos, however, you may find that your album doesn't look "right." You may feel you have too much text.

Use the following ideas to integrate the narratives into your pages:

■ **Write or print the many cameo narratives on photo-safe paper**–no other kind is appropriate for your albums. Insert pages with text between pages with photos. You can label photos and corresponding cameo narratives with the same number to match the two. Interleaving text pages between photo pages is effective if you write long stories, too.

Whether you choose to write by hand or by computer, you can vary the style of your layout and size of lettering. Writing or printing, you can vary the length of lines and the shapes of text blocks from page to page, or from album to album.

Creating text-only or text-dominant pages doesn't mean you have to give up on unique page layout designs.

Your album is a book, after all. As you design, be sure to look critically at books and magazines that come your way. What elements please you? The symmetry and balance that visual uniformity creates over the span of one album or a series of albums will allow the storyline to dominate.

Well-placed variations add flavor–titles askew or blocks at an angle draw attention. If you make variety the rule, however, watch out for the busyness and the clutter of too many jazzy designs. Too many styles and shapes on one page can detract from the story.

■ **Write directly on your album pages or insert text pages into your album.** Whether you write by hand or by computer, you can create text pages with empty blocks for the later addition of photos. The photos accompany and illustrate the text around them.

■ **Design a marginal column either for the photos or the text.**

■ **Use expandable albums into which you can insert additional pages anywhere–whether photos or text.** When you use an expandable album, you can insert narrative pages between photo pages. Be sure to label each photo (with a number system, for instance) and each cameo narrative correspondingly. Interleaving with parchment or tissue (like that of wedding invitations) between written and photo pages will protect the photographs from scuffing.

Points to Remember

■ When you have many photos, choose the ones that tell the most of your story and have the best photographic quality.

■ When you have only a few photos, supplement them with stand-alone cameo narratives to carry the storyline.

■ When you place photos and cameos together in your albums, choose design elements that favor both.

Appendices

Appendix A

The Whole Story—Even If It's The Truth?

It may seem a simple matter: of course, you'll tell the truth! But it's inevitable that sooner or later you'll encounter a decision about **what** to tell and **how** to tell it-and there'll be no simple answer in sight!

Do you really want to write, for example, that the smiling woman in the background was your father's mistress? How do you say that your cousin who left town quickly was not really an embezzler-do you write that he was merely a sloppy bookkeeper?

When you speak to relatives about your common ancestors or when you check documents and records, do you learn that the story you've always believed to be true is not at all? You may conclude that someone has lied or not been entirely frank. In choosing what version to preserve, follow your heart and keep these guidelines in mind.

Write the story your intuition tells you is true. Or choose not to tell the story at all.

1. Your unhappy memories also need to be verified. Ironically, we can be attached to our angry or sad memories and not want to verify them-perhaps for fear of having them disproved. Could the memory really be about you or a certain time in your life rather than about another person? A person or experience in an unhappy moment in your life may be tainted with the misery of that time.

Just as you can verify air temperature by reading a thermometer so, too, can you verify life facts–even the sadness–by consulting the right gauges: relatives, documents (letters, diaries, newspaper accounts, certificates, diplomas), and public records (birth and death certificates, census reports, and tax bills, among others).

"Of all that is written, I love only what a person has written with his blood."

—Nietzsche

2. Your own version of the truth may depend on

your point of view. Point of view refers to the "eyes" of the narrator from which the story is seen or understood. Your point of view always limits and colors what you know and consider to be true. But you may decide that there are other ways of looking at things besides yours–all or none of which may reflect what really happened or what you want to believe happened.

How Much Is Too Much?

When you want to–or feel you should–tell the truth, how much is too much–both for you and for your viewers? Keep the following in mind:

1. Concealing information can significantly alter a reader's interpretation of the life, theme, and events your lifestory photo album portrays. You risk lying to your family when you knowingly keep the truth hidden from them.

An instance of this, in one of the famous published diaries of the twentieth century, is Anaïs Nin's celebration of the freedoms of her life as an artist. She did not say, however, that she wasn't living off income from her own writing but was being bankrolled by a husband–a fact she never mentions, not even once! Her *Diary*, if it had included this detail, might have spared many young writers the pain (and disappointment) of modeling their lives on one they thought she was living!

In withholding an important piece of information as you record family history, might you be doing a disservice to your readers as Nin did to hers?

2. Photoscribing is not your opportunity to attack or expose anyone! Being the author doesn't give you permission to conscript someone for your side of an argument. When someone tries to engage you on his side, don't you feel that he's taking advantage of your good will? Your family will feel the same as they read your vengeful (or tell-all) cameos–especially in an album you offer them as a gift!

Exposing someone when no good can come from it is also a questionable photoscribing practice. Next to a picture of your sister, you just don't need to write:

> Here's Annie before her secret marriage. What a mess that was! She and her husband ran up credit cards like crazy...

If you know it will hurt someone close to you to give out certain information in your album, why do it?

3. You don't have to write anything you don't feel comfortable telling. You have the right to privacy. Your albums don't have to reveal details that you don't want to share.

Maintaining relationships and your dignity as a person may be more productive than telling all. Your albums, one can safely state, are not the place to confront uncomfortable or compromising truths. Setting appropriate boundaries is not only perfectly ok, it is also desirable and necessary.

Points to Remember

- Telling the truth is not a simple matter.
- Unhappy memories need to be checked just as much as happier ones.
- Don't allow yourself to use photoscribing as an opportunity to attack someone.
- You always have a right to remain silent.

Appendix B

Unsettling Memories

Recording your lifestory by photoscribing your albums will stimulate your imagination to reenter a world that no longer exists-the world of your past. Sometimes this experience brings pleasure and you welcome the memories. At other times, however, the memories are disturbing and unwelcome. Perhaps it is not a specific memory that surfaces as you look at your photos, but a faint sadness, a vague unease.

"My family's all gone now. It's hard creating a lifestory photo album without their input."

Not Just the Happy Moments

Photographs are generally taken of happy moments, occasions of family and personal celebrations when smiles are on every face.

As you spread out pictures, perhaps for the first time in years, you may relive scenes with parents and siblings, children, spouses, friends, or partners. You revisit the world portrayed in your photos. Suddenly, unannounced, unwelcome, comes a memory you had forgotten or kept at bay. Perhaps it's of poverty, or abuse, abandonment, fail-

"It's odd—I thought my childhood memories were all bad. But as I wrote cameos, I realized my parents just did their best, but they weren't really cut out to be parents."

ure, or addiction, illness, or loss. Or, you begin to think of missed opportunities and decisions not made, of relationships allowed to go bad. Something in a photo-or what it reminds you of-jumps out at you. Perhaps as you linger with a photo taken at your tenth birthday party, you see there the neighbor or family friend or place that played a role in a painful dispute or loss. The memory ambushes you after all this time.

"I am a survivor. I've worked hard to limit the ripple effect of my long, unhappy childhood. I can still remember it—but without any of the gripping anger I used to feel."

■ **The part of you still hurt by this memory is the child, not the adult, self.** Your child self, by its very nature, feels abandoned, neglected, and undervalued. (We all carry with us this resident child and can be dominated by it no matter what our age.) Your adult self, on the other hand, is always capable of protecting, nurturing, and helping. (That part of ourselves is with us whatever our age-even as children.)

Only you can assess your comfort level with unsettling memories. You do not have to take them on just now if you don't want to.

■ **You can choose to keep your child part in perspective and your adult part in control.** Let your adult speak reassuringly to your child self: "I know reliving this is difficult. I am here and I will keep you safe. You don't have to be with this person or in this circumstance ever again." Or, "This is painful, but you are safe here in the present."

■ **Make the positive choice not to let negative feelings and thoughts dominate you.** If you let them drift away from your active attention, their intensity will diminish in time. Coming across the photo of an individual who wronged you may fill you with helpless anger. But you are not helpless now. You can choose a strategy that ensures you are not overtak-

"I'm not that way now. It's unpleasant to go back and see the person I was then."

en once again; let those negative thoughts go (no matter how justified). Practicing this habit helps you move on.

An Effective Tool

Writing is an effective and powerful tool for working through difficult memories. Creating lifestory albums may help you to come to terms with sadness and discomfort. While the experience of photoscribing painful memories isn't pleasant, it can help you to do the following:

■ **understand what happened.** For some people, knowledge can lead to release.

■ **diminish negative feelings.** When memories are worked with in a non-judgmental way, they lose their intense charge of feeling. Holding on can keep them burning.

■ **let go of anger.** Sometimes it is helpful to vent sorrow or pain on paper (but not necessarily to share that writing). After such a catharsis, we feel better.

The process of dealing with unsettling memories is more significant than producing finished albums. Deal honestly with painful life details first. Then decide whether or not to share them.

Accepting a painful or sad experience can transform you from a victim into a person who is ready to move on. In this healing, your writing is a confidante, an ideal listener.

The Indirect Approach

You can best approach some pain indirectly. For instance, if the death of a loved one is still too raw, try organizing photos about other people, events, or eras she or he was not central to. Eventually, like peeling an onion, layer by layer, you will begin to approach the center of your grief—and move towards acceptance and understanding. As you do so, you will find yourself writing about this person with greater ease and you may even allow yourself to re-experience more pleasant memories of them, too.

Photoscribing is not a substitute for counseling if you are dealing with trauma. But there are therapeutic benefits to reviewing and writing about your past.

When you feel ready, begin to work with the photos you associate with pain or discomfort in your past and give preserving your difficult stories a try.

Points to Remember

- Making a heritage lifestory album is likely to bring up some unsettling memories for most of us.
- Photoscribing is an effective tool for dealing with emotional pain. It is not, however, a substitute for counseling or therapy.
- Dealing with pain indirectly is a viable choice.

Appendix C

Sample Cameo Narratives

In the following examples I have written for a biographical heritage album about my father, I use long cameo narratives to fill in the gaps between photos. Even if I had more photos, they couldn't tell the whole story that needs to be told in these cameos. Only the addition of cameo narratives and informative captions can fill the gap between photographs and life as it was lived.

These two cameo narratives depend on dialogue for their development. The first is a transcript of two conversations. It appears on a page which features photos of my father and me. In one of these, for instance, he is holding me, age 10 months, on his knee, in the fall of 1947. He's wearing an overcoat and I am all bundled up in a hooded one-piece suit.

"Why didn't Dad take advantage of the GI Bill?" Mom asked me in 1998. "He was a smart man. He could have gotten a good job for himself if he'd gotten a degree then. A lot of fellows did that when they got out of the service after the war. It just didn't interest him that much, I guess."

I remember my grandmother saying to me when I was an adolescent, "We had the money to help him then, just before the war. He could have stayed in school. He didn't want to."

This cameo narrative reveals something about my father that is not seen in the photo of the young man holding his baby son on his lap. Yet it is important information. At the time of this picture, undetected by the camera, his decision not to pursue further education was one that would have serious consequences for him and his family. The cameo narrative explains him and, with others, creates a portrait that would otherwise be lost. It's part of his–and consequently my–larger story, and I want to preserve it in my album.

The second cameo narrative is not about the character of an individual but a community. It is a remembered version of a conversation in which my father himself "speaks." I transcribed this conversation from memory many years after it was spoken.

> "When I was little, we lived down on Bates Street (part of the tenement district)," my father told me. "Children didn't misbehave. They knew they couldn't without everyone knowing. If a kid was naughty, a mother in a nearby apartment would throw a window open and stick her head out, 'Go home right now. What do you think you're doing? You know better than that! I'll see your mother tonight at the Ladies of St. Anne! She's going to be mad when she hears about this!'"

The photos I have of my father include those of his First Communion and of his confirmation, but I have none of him in daily activity in the district where he grew up. I include the previous cameo narrative among the photos of celebratory moments because I want to tell the full story of what his childhood was like. The woman who flung open the window didn't doubt for a moment that other mothers would welcome her intervention. She expected the same from them.

Photoscribing allows his grandchildren and their children to learn that communities in their grandfather's day were cohesive and not at all anonymous.

Here are two more cameo narratives that fill a story gap in my photo album. They come from a Lifelist I did for my father's life. They feature setting. In them, I describe in two separate ways the neighborhood to which my father moved as an adolescent. It was uptown in an area of single homes with little yards.

> The Farwell Street neighborhood reflected a change as mill workers moved out of downtown to outlying districts. In 1936, these areas of town were developing fast. Holy Family parish had been organized in 1923 but it was still celebrating its liturgy out of a basement church on Sabattus Street.

> For my Grandmother Ledoux, Holy Family was always a temporary parish, not a fit replacement in her heart for the huge, gothic Sts. Peter and Paul whose spires dominated the downtown skyline after its completion in 1938. She had contributed regularly to its construction and had followed the liturgy there since 1916.

This cameo narrative tells you something about both the neighborhood at that time and my grandmother. The next one focuses more specifically on my father's neighborhood.

> The Farwell Street neighborhood may have been far from the city's cramped downtown but it was still full of family.
>
>
>
> Highland Avenue was perpendicular to Farwell Street. Dad's aunt (his mother's sister) Rosilia and her husband, Thomas Beaulieu, lived there in a house almost identical to the Ledouxs'. They had two sons, René and Roland, who were Dad's age. Then, two houses away was another, older cousin, Rosa

Rioux Labourdais (her mother was Dad's aunt and godmother, Ernestine Bilodeau Rioux). Rosa lived there with her husband and children. Four houses beyond lived another cousin, Albert Lizotte, (his mother was Dad's aunt, Angéline Bilodeau Lizotte) with his wife Aline and daughter Fernande.

Later, when Dad married the girl next door, he added to his neighborhood a set of parents-in-law and an uncle and aunt-in-law (Albin and Augustine Lambert Lessard).

These cameo narratives are on a page with photos of the Ledouxs on their lawn at 49 Farwell St. They are the only photos I have of this period so I use narrative text to reveal key elements of the setting that a photo of smiling relatives in the yard can't.

The next example, by contrast, features an action to convey its portrait.

In the mornings (before he moved out to Farwell Street in 1936), William walked from his apartment to the Bates Mill with the thousands of other operatives who descended from their tenements–in the cold dark of winter, in the cool light of summer–to fill the street. People came for the seven o'clock shift from New Auburn across the river, from the narrow, twisted streets of Little Canada, and from the neighborhood north of the park where the apartments were larger, more modern, and expensive. Workers filled the streets on their way to the Bates, the Hill, the Androscoggin, and the Pepperell along the canal and to the Continental by the Androscoggin River.

This photo was taken c. 1960. *Pépère* was a foreman at the Bates Mill for 42 years.

In the afternoon, at 2:45, the workers flooded the streets again as men and women came for the second shift–the latecomers rubbing shoulders with the first shift who trudged home beginning at three for an early supper and rest.

Each example features one aspect but includes others, too. The above narrative is based on an action, but is strong on setting. The following is also an action-based narrative with a strong emphasis on setting.

In those days before road salting and modern plows, Bartlett Hill was closed for the winter. The tenement children gathered on cold, bright afternoons to slide. Bartlett was a clear, steep hill that started where Androscoggin Avenue is today. From there, you could see the towers of City Hall and St. Patrick's Church (but not yet Sts. Peter and Paul, which was completed only in 1938). As my father grew up, the construction continued and the church with its gothic spires rose over the city—every year a more spectacular cityscape to see from Bartlett Hill. Their sled ride ended at Mailhot's Sausage at the bottom, a long exhilarating run that would be the subject of many animated conversations the next day during recess at St. Peter's School.

Resources Appendix

Glossary

action: see plot.

annotate: to complement with short, explanatory written material. Photoscribes use captions to do this.

autobiography: an account of the writer's own life; often used interchangeably with the terms *memoir* and *lifestory*.

background: the part of a photo situated behind the subject(s) which are depicted, as opposed to *foreground*.

biography: the written account of the life of another person; often used interchangeably with *memoir* and *lifestory*.

cameo narratives: short lifestory narratives, generally 50 to 150 words–although they can be shorter or longer.

caption (photo caption): information labels placed near photos as brief phrases or bulleted lists; also called *annotations*.

cast of characters: the "actors" or people who are central to the photo caption, cameo narrative, lifestory photo album.

cliché: a trite, stereotyped expression that has lost originality and effect by long overuse. It usually contains a kernel of truth but its shorthand often misses the mark.

colloquial: characteristic of familiar or everyday conversation rather than of formal speech or writing.

dialogue: a conversation between two or more persons. Can also be internal. (I said to myself, "Why?")

edit: to correct a text for grammar and spelling and to check for consistency, coherence, completeness, and conciseness.

extended lifelist: a lifelist which contains the memories of an entire lifetime.

foreground: the front and often the focus or subject of the photo, as opposed to *background;* most often what we want to preserve.

lifelist: a list of any and all memories of people, events, feelings, longings, etc.; includes both the Extended and the limited lifelist. Also called Memory List.

lifestory: a story of a life, usually created in independent segments which do not need to be linked with one another as in an autobiography; often used interchangeably with *autobiography, biography,* and *memoir.*

lifestory photo album: a photo album, composed of narrative text and photos, that tells an autobiography or a biography.

limited lifelist: a lifelist which contains the memories of a specific event, theme, or era.

memoir: a part of an autobiography dealing specifically with presenting a comprehensive view of a time or activity; often used interchangeably with *autobiography, biography,* and *lifestory.*

musings: ruminations or "what if" thoughts that reveal the writer's internal or imaginative life.

narrative: an account of events and experiences told in prose. In a lifestory album, narrative is told in photographs, in words, or in a combination of both.

phonetic transcription: dialogue which records conversation or speech according to pronunciation rather than correct or standard spelling and grammar.

photo caption: see "caption."

photo safe: acid-free and lignin-free as well as ph neu-tral and stable; high quality materials that will not destroy your narratives and photos over time are photo safe.

photoscribing: the process of writing expressive texts and combining them with photographs in order to create a lifestory photo album.

plot (action): the action of the story.

re-write: to fine tune, improve, and re-work texts for clarity, feeling, and description. To rewrite is to revise.

rough draft: the first, raw text which will be rewritten and edited.

setting: the surroundings and environment as well as the culture and time period in which the story of your text takes place.

storyline: A synonym for narrative.

vignette: a short, meaningful narrative; a self-contained mini-story.

voice: the authentic quality and character of a particular personality; in writing: authenticity of representation.

Bibliography

I have found the following writing books helpful to myself and to my lifewriting students. This is not a comprehensive list.

Albert, Susan Wittig. *Writing From Life / Telling Your Soul's Story*, Jeremy Tharcher/Putnam, NY, NY. 1996. *More process—rather than finished product—oriented.*

Franco, Carol and Lineback, Kent. *The Legacy Guide*, Jeremy Tarcher, NY, NY. 2006. *Many exercises and suggestions for capturing the facts, memories, and meaning of your life.*

Hagberg, Janet O. *Wrestling with Your Angels / A Spiritual Journey to Great Writing*, Adams Publishing, Holbrook, MA. 1995. *Exercises to deepen awareness and discipline through the craft of writing.*

Kempthorne, Charlie. *For All Time / A Complete Guide to Writing Your Family History*, Boynton/Cook/Heinemann, Portsmouth, NH. 1996. *Covers much of the same ground as my* Turning Memories Into Memoirs. *A good read. Accessible.*

Kowit, Steve. *In the Palm of Your Hand / The Poet's Portable Workshop*, Tilbury House, Gardiner, ME. 1995. *A lively guide for the practicing poet and for those interested in perfecting style.*

Maisel, Eric. *Fearless Creating / A Step-by-Step Guide to Starting and Completing Your Work of Art*, Jeremy Tharcher/Putnam, NY, NY. 1995. *This book is masterful in making clear and accessible each step of the creative process; for the serious creative.*

Rosenbluth, Vera. *Keeping Family Stories Alive,* Hartley & Marks, Point Roberts WA & Vancoouver, BC. 1997. *A focus on the oral aspect of lifestory preservation.*

Scrapbook Guild. *The Simple Art of Scrapbooking*, The Scrapbook Guild/Dell Paperback, NY, NY. 1998. *An excellent book for creative treatment of scrapbook form and content. Not a writing book, but a page layout book; of special interest to photoscribes.*

Selling, Bernard. *Writing from Within / A Guide to Creativity and Life Story Writing*, Hunter House, Alameda, CA. 1998. *Especially for those who want writing to lead them deeper. Solid writing suggestions for all levels. For the serious creative.*

Soleil Press Directory

Resources for Photoscribes, Lifewriters, and Teachers

Soleil Press—

Founded in 1988 by author and teacher Denis Ledoux, Soleil Press is the publishing arm of the Soleil Lifestory Network, dedicated to producing high-quality instructional materials for people who preserve their personal and family stories through written memoirs and lifestory photograph albums.

We also offer book production services—design and pre-press preparation—for those who want to self publish their memoirs.

Publications—

Photoscribing

- **The Photo Scribe, A Writing Guide: How to Write the Stories Behind your Photographs**................19.95
- **The Photoscribe's Memory Binder** 21.95
  (a companion workbook /3-ring binder with many additional exercises to organize your photoscribing projects)
- **Photoscribe Worksheets** *(for classes)* *100 per tear-off pad:*
  Writing Great Cameo Narratives......................9.95
  Writing Great Memory Lists..............................9.95

■ **The Photo Scribe Teacher Kit**...........................129.00
(Class Lesson Plans, Step-by-Step Worksheet Pads, *The Photo Scribe*, *The Photo Scribe's Memory Binder, and more.*)

Become a Photo Scribe Teacher!

If you lead album-design and photo-preservation programs, **The Photo Scribe Teacher Kit** will enable you to add a writing component—cameo narratives and more complete captions–to your workshops. This well-structured teacher program will help you to add another income stream to your offerings.

Lifewriting

■ **Turning Memories Into Memoirs**
A Handbook for Writing Lifestories.................24.95
■ **The Lifewriter's Memory Binder** 21.95
(custom 3-ring binder to organize your lifewriting projects)
■ **The Turning Memories Audio Guide** 16.95
excerpts from the Handbook in a 120-minute, two-tape set)

Ordering Information

Please call or visit www.turningmemories.com for shipping and handling charges. We accept orders by phone, email, or mail; you may pay with a major credit card, PayPal, personal check, purchase order or money order.

207–353–5454
(9 AM – 5 PM, EST)

Visit our website:
www.turningmemories.com

Materials For Lifewriting Workshop Leaders

Affiliate & Associate Teacher Packages

(Please inquire for details: packages include your web listing and network support materials: Handbook, Audio Guide, Memory Binder, Curriculum Manual (multiple models & syllabus) plus the Presenter's Manual (a comprehensive course in effective workshop presentation), Publicity Templates, e-newsletter, volume discounts on participant materials.

Become a Lifewriting Teacher!

If you have a writing and/or teaching background, becoming an Affiliate Lifewriting Teacher could be the next step in your professional development. As a Soleil Lifestory Network Affiliate, you can earn either a full- or a part-time income doing creative work that's truly significant—for you and for your community.

The Network is an international affiliation of writing professionals in English-speaking countries and throughout the US and Canada. Affiliates are committed to and experienced in assisting people to write their personal and family stories through workshops, seminars, and programs using the Turning Memories™ and Photo Scribe methods, materials, and curricula. Many, like Denis Ledoux, offer writer coaching, editing and co-authoring services, too.

We invite you to contact us for more information about how our comprehensive and well-proven materials can launch or revitalize your memoir career.

Index

Notes

When I was five we lived in the house on the hill. It was a magical place, an old New England farmhouse surrounded by a nine acre wood and high grassy meadow overlooking the river and the town. On the river side, the land tumbled away down a cliff—a craggy granite ledge which a former owner had equipped with a Victorian iron railing and a crudely cut path and steps. I would imagine I was one of the ladies with a parasol in my grandmother's photographs as I tripped along the path in delicately heeled high-button shoes, carrying the train of my traveling costume. It was our favorite way to reach the road below and provided wonderful sites for hide-and-seek. Deep in the wood was a mica mine— treasure in the heart of darkness. Standing behind the house a row of tall pines—giant pines to a five-year-old—a broad swing with ropes reaching up into the sky. The smell of pine needles and the sense of height, the soaring whoosh of pine boughs, and the dizzy motion of ecstatic swinging all come